YOU CAN TEACH YOURSELF

BANJO

By Janet Davis

A stereo cassette tape of the music in this book is now available. The publisher strongly recommends the use of this cassette tape along with the text to insure accuracy of interpretation and ease in learning.

MEL BAY ®

Contents

It's Fun!!!

The five-string banjo is a fascinating instrument and a lot of fun to play. Although it may seem impossible to play all of those notes, you will find that, surprisingly, it is not that difficult to learn, and no previous musical knowledge is needed. I have taught 5-year-olds and 80-year-olds, and they all have a good time pickin' and grinnin.'

The whole key to playing the banjo is to realize that the right hand is using specific fingering patterns to play every song. Once you learn these patterns, you can play any song using the same patterns with the right hand, while the left hand holds chord positions.

There are only four basic right-hand patterns. These are called **roll patterns.** If you learn these to the point that you can easily and spontaneously play each "roll," you will find that they become like old friends, and you will recognize each one as you come across it in different arrangements of songs.

A roll pattern is a picking order for the right fingers and consists of eight notes (equal to one measure of music). You can hold any chord with the left hand and play the same roll pattern with the right hand. These give a song that "bluegrass feeling."

Learn to play each of the roll patterns and learn its name.

The left hand works from chord positions. The same chords are used for many different songs. (Open strings will often be used for the G chord because the banjo is tuned to a G chord.)

All of this will make more sense as you work through each lesson.

But first you need to learn to tune your banjo. . . .

The Banjo

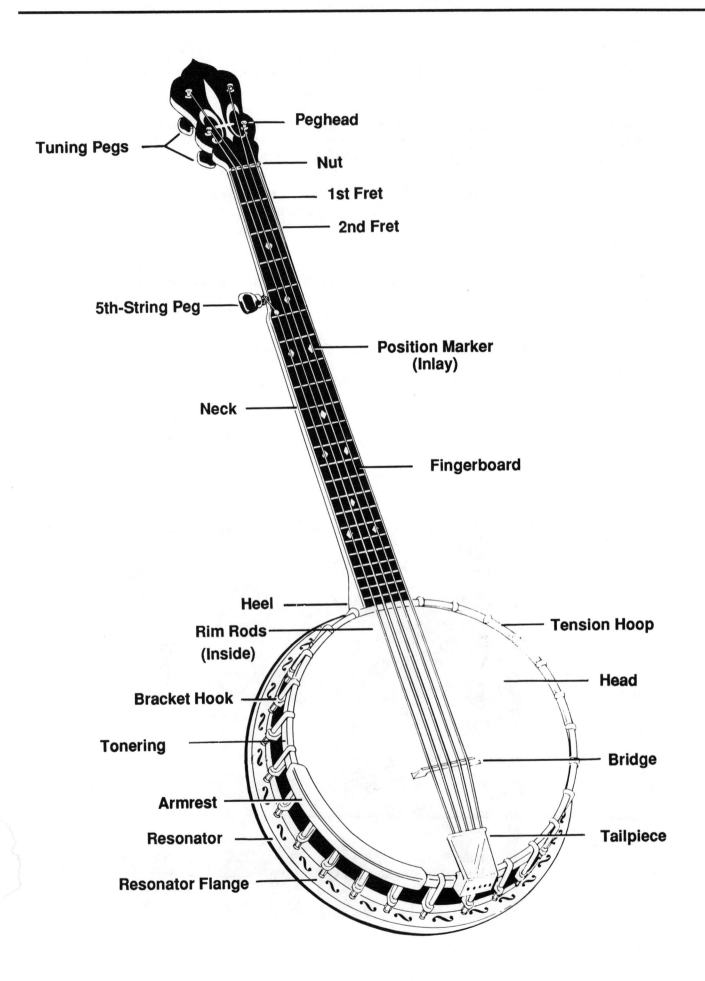

Tuning Pegs

Peghead

Nut

1st Fret

2nd Fret

5th-String Peg

Position Marker
(Inlay)

Neck

Fingerboard

Heel

Rim Rods
(Inside)

Tension Hoop

Bracket Hook

Head

Tonering

Bridge

Armrest

Resonator

Tailpiece

Resonator Flange

Lesson 1A: Tuning the Banjo

G Tuning

The G tuning is the most common tuning used for three-finger picking. The banjo can be tuned to itself without using another instrument:

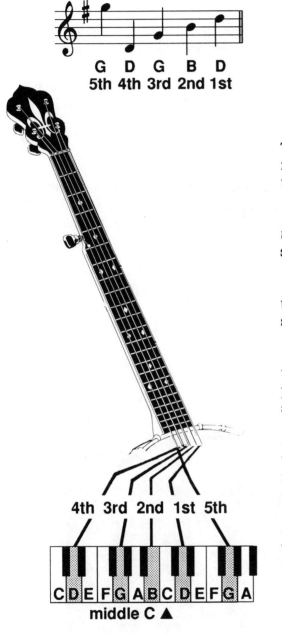

G   D   G   B   D
5th 4th 3rd 2nd 1st

4th 3rd 2nd 1st 5th

C D E F G A B C D E F G A
middle C ▲

1. *The strings are numbered in order:*
   The fifth string is the short string **(G)**.
   The fourth string is next to the fifth string **(D)**.
   The third string is the middle string **(G)**.
   The second string is next **(B)**.
   The first string is closest to the floor **(D)**.

2. To tune your banjo, *start with the fourth string.* This string is the *deepest tone on your banjo.* It is normally tuned to a **D** (below middle C on the piano). All of the other strings will be tuned in relation to this string.

3. Depress the *fourth string at the 5th fret,* and *tune the third string* to this pitch **(G).** The open third string sounds like the fourth string fretted at the 5th fret.

4. Depress the *third string on the 4th fret* and tune the *second string* to this pitch **(B).** The open second string sounds like the third string fretted at the 4th fret.

5. Hold the *second string on the 3rd fret* and tune the *first string* to this pitch **(D** next to middle C on the piano). The open first string sounds like the second string fretted on the 3rd fret.

6. Depress the *first string at the 5th fret* and tune the *fifth string* to this pitch **(G** above middle C). The open fifth string sounds like the first string, 5th fret.

When tuned correctly, the strings will sound a G chord when strummed. **Also:** The first and fourth strings will sound in unison, an octave apart (D's); the third and fifth strings should sound alike, an octave apart (G's).

NOTES
---

1. A piano or a pitch pipe will help. Electronic tuners are also now available which are easy to use and automatically tell you when each string is in tune.

2. (Hint): If a string is out of tune and you can't tell if it is too high or too low . . . loosen the string first, then tune it. This way you will know it is low, and you can tighten it until it is in tune. (And you won't break the string by going toooooo high.)

3. The left fingers should press the strings down between the metal bars, not directly on the bar.

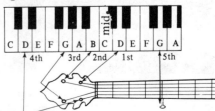

C D E F G A B C D E F G A
        4th   3rd 2nd 1st   5th

Lesson 1B: Holding the Banjo

Looking good is the first step to sounding good!! (Even if you don't know what you are doing, a lot of people will think you do.)

Have a good time, and your listeners will, too!

- Relax, but . . .

- Sit up straight if you are seated. Stand up straight if you are standing.

- Hold the banjo upright. Do not lay the banjo flat on your lap.

- The peghead should be about level with your left shoulder.

- A strap (preferably all leather) will aid in holding the banjo securely. You can wear it over either shoulder. (It will feel more secure over your left shoulder, over your head.)

- Your left hand holds the neck. The thumb usually wraps around to the other side. However, it will also move around and give the fingers support by pressing against the back of the neck.

- The right hand picks the strings over the head.

Lesson 1C: The Right Hand

Only three fingers are used for picking the banjo: thumb, index finger, and the middle finger.

How to Wear Fingerpicks

You will need three picks:

- A plastic thumbpick
- Two metal fingerpicks

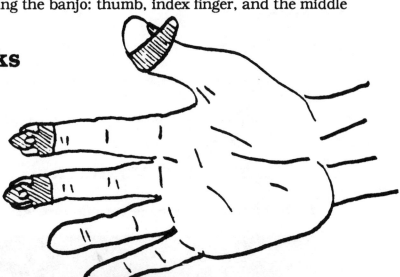

Thumbpick (plastic):

- The point should aim toward the head of the banjo, not up in the air.

- The curve should be around the fingernail side of the thumb. The straight side is on the flesh side of the thumb.

Fingerpicks:

- Wear one on your *index finger* and on your *middle finger* (right hand).

- Wear the curved part along the flesh side of your finger, not the fingernail side!

- Bend the picks to fit snugly.

- The picks should extend about ⅛″ from the tips of your fingers.

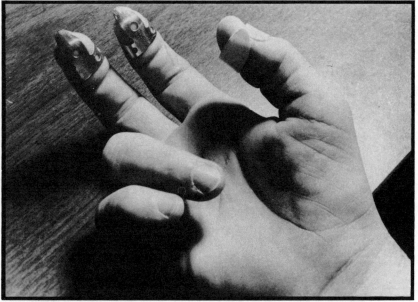

- ***Place the picks on your fingers so they pick the strings on the flat side . . . not at an angle.*** (If at an angle, they will squeak on the strings.)

- ***Picks are a personal choice*** (experiment). Most professionals use a fairly stiff thumbpick (plastic). For a beginner, any plastic thumbpick will get you started, but it should fit fairly snugly.

- Often, a thumbpick won't fit snugly. Reshape it by holding it in hot water and molding it. It should fit tightly enough so that it doesn't slip around.

- The metal fingerpicks will not feel comfortable at first. However, eventually you will probably prefer them. The heavier gauged metal picks provide more tone from your banjo.

- A short extension from the end of your finger may provide easier playing. A longer extension provides a crisper tone . . . less finger, more pick touches the string.

- For more picking power, some people wrap the fingerpick flush around the tip of the finger.

- Experiment for comfort and tone.

Lesson 1D: Picking the Banjo

Picking

Pick the banjo with three fingers only:

• The thumb plucks down, toward the floor.

• The two fingers (index and middle) pluck up, toward the ceiling.

The Right-Hand Position

Right-hand placement is very important:

• Brace your **little finger** against the head (drum), right in front of the bridge. **Note:** Do not place it on the bridge, for it will dampen the tone of your banjo.

• Your ring finger should eventually be held down, too, but beginners need not worry about this.

•**Important:** Pick the strings over the head, in front of the bridge with three fingers: the thumb, index, and middle fingers of the right hand.

• At first you may want to watch your right hand, in order to pick the correct strings. Try to avoid watching your right hand as time goes on, or it will slow down your playing.

• It is better to watch your left hand than your right hand. It is better yet to look at your audience. *Make it look EASY.*

——————— NOTES ———————

1. Pick with short strokes.

2. T = Thumb; I = Index; M = Middle.

Lesson 1E: Tablature

Tablature is a simple system designed for those who do not read music. It can be learned in a few minutes. Basically, it is comprised of lines, numbers, and stems.

• The five lines are the five strings of your banjo. Each line represents a particular string.

• The numbers are fret numbers; they tell you which fret to hold down with the left hand on a particular string.

For example: "2" on the top line tells you to fret (hold down) the 2nd fret on the first string. "3" on the middle line means to fret the 3rd fret on the third string. "0" means to pick the string open (without fretting it).

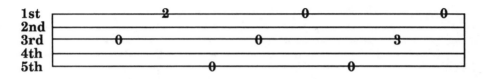

Summary

• The *lines* tell you which *string* to pick; the *numbers* tell you which *fret number* to hold (on that string) with the left hand.

• The *lines* are the five *strings* of your banjo.

• The *numbers* are *fret numbers.* 4

• *Two numbers,* one over the other, $\begin{smallmatrix}0\\3\end{smallmatrix}$ are to be played at the *same time*. This is called a **pinch.**

• Right-Hand Fingers: T = Thumb; I = Index; M = Middle. (Only three fingers pick the strings.)

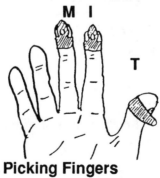

Picking Fingers

NOTES

Push the string down *between* the metal fret bars, not on the metal bar.

Rhythm

The **duration,** or length of time each note should *ring,* is indicated by the **stem,** or line which is drawn from each number. This is referred to as the **rhythm** or the **timing.**

Good timing is very important when playing the banjo.

♪ The basic unit in banjo music is called an **eighth note.**

There will be eight eighth notes in one measure of tablature.

Each eighth note should receive equal duration. **Do not hold one note longer than another.**

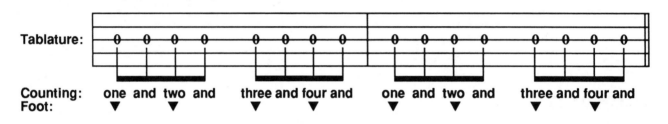

Two measures of eighth notes should be picked evenly, without stopping between the measures. The listener should not know there are divisions in your tablature. This is only for your (reading) convenience when learning to play the song.

♩ The next most common unit is a **quarter note.**

The quarter note is held (should ring) twice as long as an eighth note. Hold for the duration of two eighth notes.

♩ = ♫

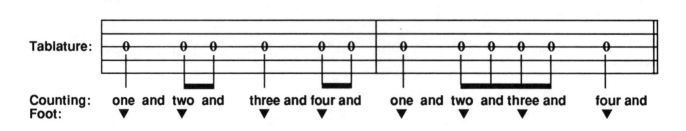

♪ The **sixteenth note.**

Play two sixteenth notes for the duration of one eighth note. (Play four sixteenth notes for the duration of one quarter note.)

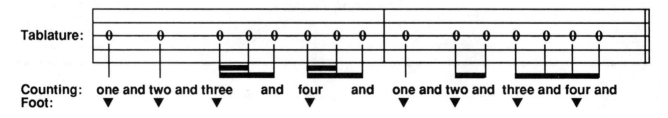

Lesson 2: Roll Patterns

Introduction

Roll patterns are the basis for all songs played in Scruggs style on the banjo. Every song you play will be comprised of various combinations of roll patterns. *There are only four basic patterns to learn.* Everything else you play can be traced to one of these.

• **Definition:** A roll pattern is a right-hand fingering (picking) pattern. The order or sequence in which the right-hand fingers follow one another when they pick the strings determines the name of each pattern.

For example: *The forward roll* = I M T I M T I M (notice the fingering order or pattern):

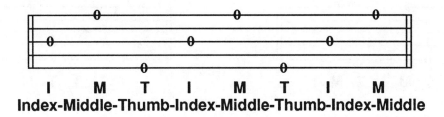

I M T I M T I M
Index-Middle-Thumb-Index-Middle-Thumb-Index-Middle

Actually, this pattern can begin with any finger, but the picking sequence must remain the same — e.g. thumb follows middle finger.

• *Each pattern consists of eight eighth notes* (one measure of music or tablature).

• Each roll pattern can be played while holding *any chord* with the left hand. Each of the roll-pattern examples on the following page is written using only open strings (no left-hand action is required). Practice them this way first. Once you are comfortable with each pattern, you can hold any chord position with the left hand while you pick each pattern with the right hand.

• When you play songs using these patterns, generally the finger which begins or starts the pattern will pick melody notes, while the other two fingers play background, or harmony notes.

• *You can also practice these patterns on a table or on the steering wheel when you are driving. A banjo is not necessary to train the right hand.*

──────────────── NOTES ────────────────

All of this will make more sense as you progress through the book.

The Basic Roll Patterns

1. Forward Roll (I M T I M T I M) Variation (begin with thumb)

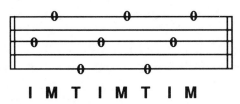

   I M T I M T I M

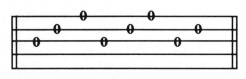

   T I M T I M T I

2. Backward Roll (M I T M I T M I) Variation (begin with index)

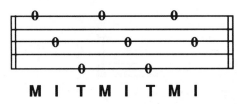

   M I T M I T M I

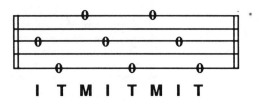

   I T M I T M I T

3. Forward-Reverse Roll (T I M T M I T M) Variation (begin with fifth string)
(Go forward, then backward)

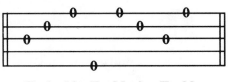

   T I M T M I T M

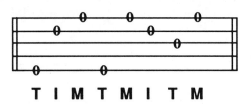

   T I M T M I T M

4. Mixed Roll or Alternating-Thumb Roll Variation (same right-hand pattern)

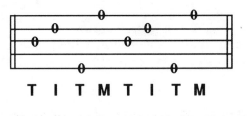

   T I T M T I T M

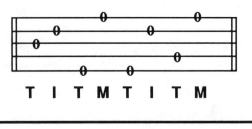

   T I T M T I T M

--- NOTES ---

1. The forward-roll and backward-roll patterns can begin with any finger: T I M T I M T I is also a forward roll. The order the fingers follow one another determines the name of the roll pattern.

2. With the forward roll, you may have a tendency to play nine notes, including an extra note. Each roll pattern has only eight notes.

3. At the end of the pattern you can begin the same pattern again, or you can play a different pattern.

4. Practice playing each pattern with a steady rhythm — EVENLY. Repeat each pattern over and over, without a break in your rhythm.

5. Learn the name of each pattern. (Notice right-hand fingering.)

6. With experience, you will learn to recognize these patterns upon hearing them.

7. *Use these patterns as warm-up exercises from now on!*

Lesson 3: Chords

When playing the banjo, the left hand usually works from chord positions, while the right hand picks the strings. In each song, chord symbols are indicated above the tablature. When you see a chord symbol above the tablature in a song (i.e. C), you should hold that chord position with the left hand.

To begin playing the banjo, you need to learn only three chords—the G, C, and D7 chords. These chords are used to play many different songs.

The following positions are used to play these chords in the open-string area of the banjo, from the 1st through the 5th fret. (Because the banjo is tuned to a G chord, all of the strings are left open to play this chord.)

You can play many songs on the banjo using only these three chords:

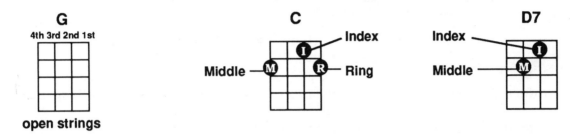

EXERCISE: *Play the mixed-roll pattern one time for each of the above chords, without stopping between chords. Try this with each of the roll patterns until you can change chords smoothly with the left hand.*

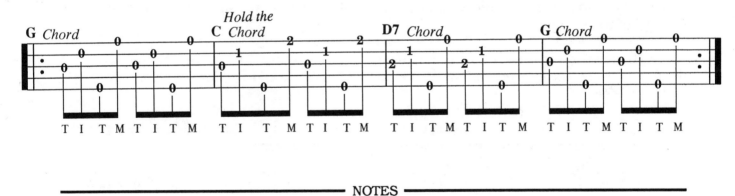

───────── NOTES ─────────

1. For the C chord only, it is not necessary to fret the fourth string if this is difficult. Later on, you can add the middle finger when this is required in a song.

2. Pay special attention to the *left-hand fingering* for each chord. This will be important for speed and for changing chords smoothly.

3. Compare the C chord with the D7 chord. Notice that the index finger stays in the same place for both chords (second string, 1st fret). The middle finger moves from the fourth to the third string when changing from C to D7.

4. The G and D chords often work with open strings.

See the back of the book for complete chord charts!

Lesson 4:
Using the Forward-Roll Pattern

The same roll pattern can be used to play an entire song, simply by playing it for each measure of the song while holding the proper chord position(s) with the left hand. The melody notes are placed as the first note of each measure. The same finger will play the melody note each time that finger picks in the pattern. (This will make sense as you begin to play the songs.)

The arrangement on the next page of "Bile Dem Cabbage Down" uses the **forward-roll pattern** as the primary roll:

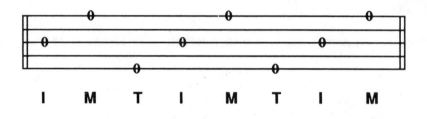

* Notice that each measure of this song contains the forward-roll pattern.

* The melody notes (tune of the song — what you might sing) are played with the *index finger* and should be emphasized (played slightly louder).

* *Do not stop* or pause between any note or at the bar lines between each measure!

* The left hand should *hold the C chord* when it is required, and the left hand should *hold the D7 chord* when it is required. (See chord symbols above the music.) *The G chord* is played with all of the strings open.

* The next-to-the-last measure shares a G and a D7 chord. Therefore, the roll pattern is divided between these chords (three notes for the G chord, and five for the D7).

* Again, notice the pattern has only eight notes.
a) Don't add an extra note at the end of each measure with the thumb; it isn't there!
b) Don't stop at the end of each pattern — keep on picking.
c) Don't stop picking when the left hand is grabbing the C chord. **Note:** If changing chords is new to you, you need to fret only the first two strings for the C chord to play this song.

The listener should not know you are playing a pattern for each measure! This may take a lot of practice.

The Forward Roll

- The forward-roll pattern is played for *every measure* in the following arrangement.

- *Hold the C chord* with the left hand when it is indicated by the chord symbol (measures 2 and 6).

- *Keep your right-hand picking steady.* Do not hesitate at the end of each roll pattern (measure) or before a chord change. (This takes practice.)

Bile Dem Cabbage Down
(The Forward Roll)

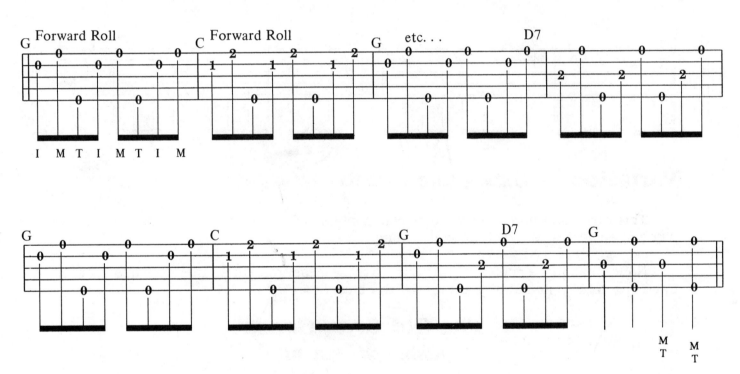

Notice that the forward-roll pattern has a "kink" or an interruption in the fingering pattern at the end of each bar line (measure). Because the roll has only eight notes, you start over at each bar line. Don't let the listener hear this.

Do not stop or hesitate at the bar line! Keep your rhythm steady (like a machine gun)!

Lesson 5: The Old Gray Goose

The same roll pattern can be used to play many different tunes. Remember to *emphasize the index finger* each time it occurs. This finger plays the melody or tune of the song while the other fingers provide harmony, based upon the chords of the song.

The Old Gray Goose
(The Forward Roll)

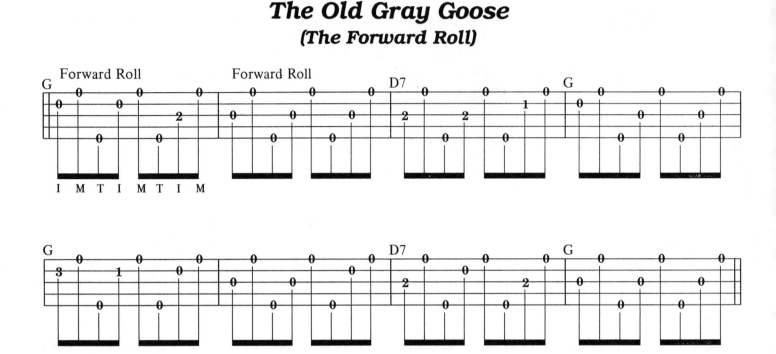

Variation — Using the Pinch

This variation utilizes the pinch, which involves picking two notes simultaneously. The pinch often serves as punctuation in a song.

Notice that quarter notes (♩) are used in these measures. Pause after each quarter note. Each one is held the duration of two eighth notes: ♩ = ♪♪ or $\frac{0}{1}$ = $\frac{0\ 0}{}$

The Old Gray Goose
(Using the Pinch)

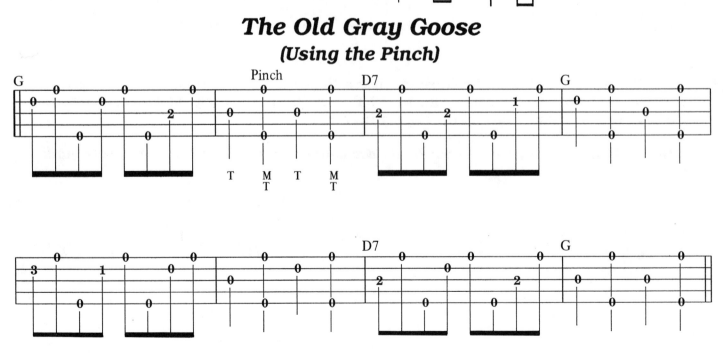

Lesson 6:
The Forward-Reverse Roll

The following variation uses the forward-reverse roll pattern for each measure: T I M T M I T M. Be careful to hold the correct chords with the left hand.

The Old Gray Goose
(Using the Forward-Reverse Roll)

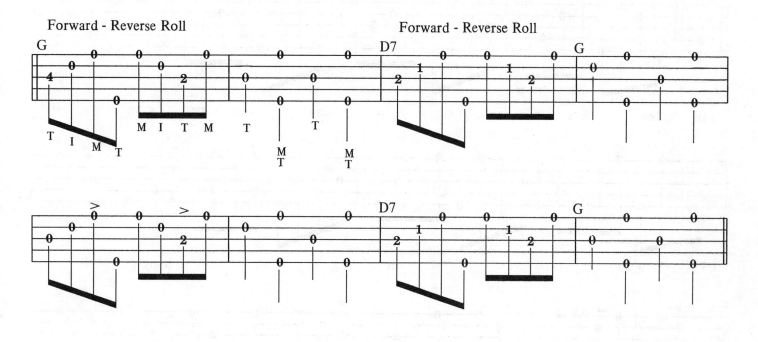

Lesson 7: Worried Man Blues

Each measure of this tune uses the forward-reverse roll pattern. Emphasize the thumb each time it occurs to bring out the melody notes.

Worried Man Blues
(Using the Forward-Reverse Roll)

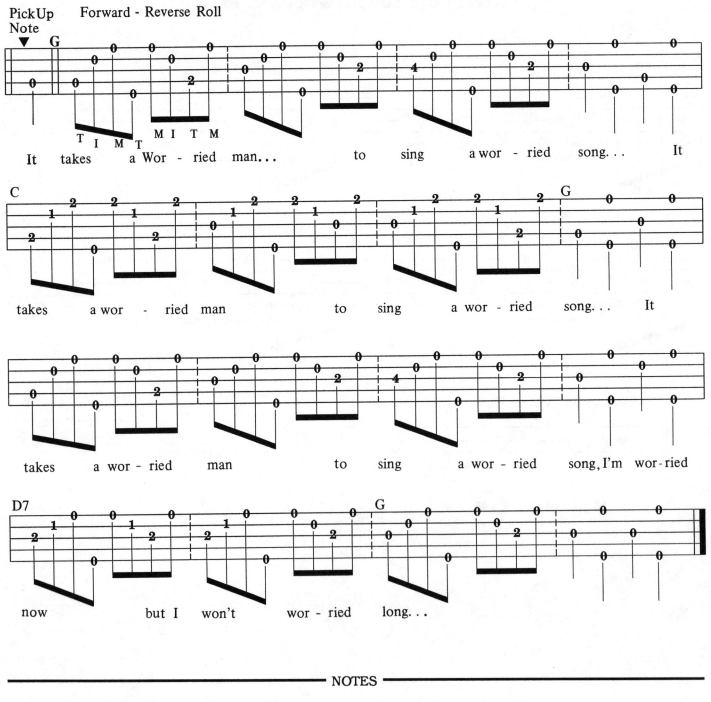

___ NOTES ___

Remember to hold the C-chord position with the left hand when this chord occurs.

Lesson 8: Mountain Dew

Notice that this arrangement is very similar to the one for "Worried Man Blues." This is because the tunes (melodies) for these songs are quite similar, and the arrangements use the same roll pattern. With experience, you will begin to use different roll patterns as you feel them for each song you play. You will also utilize left-hand techniques, which will be introduced in the next few lessons. However, you will find that many traditional songs are actually quite similar.

Mountain Dew
(Using the Forward-Reverse Roll)

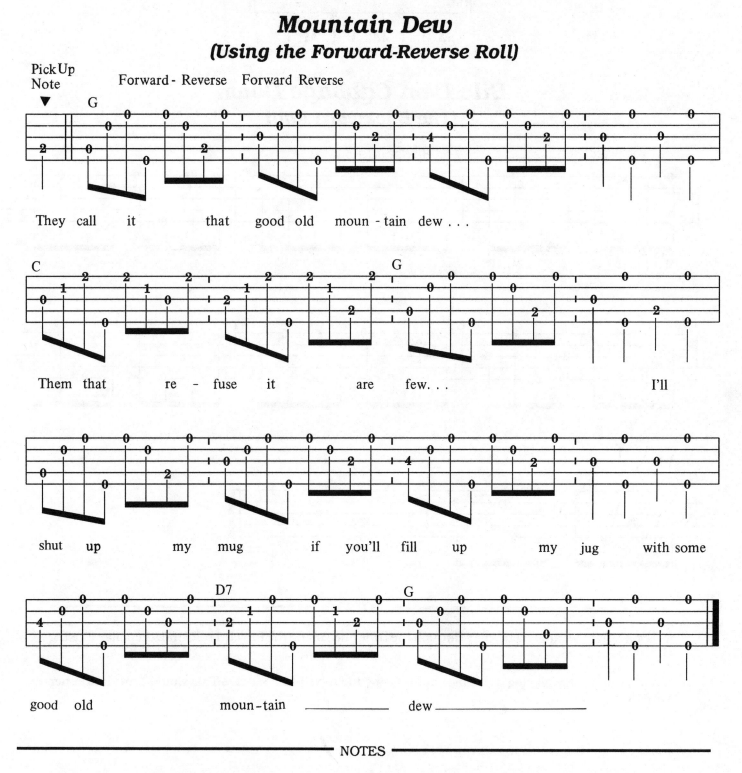

NOTES

The roll patterns will not include every melody note for a song. The less important notes are often implied. Also, the accent placement, or where the melody notes fall, may vary in each arrangement, depending upon which roll patterns are used to play a song.

Lesson 9: The Backward Roll

You can use any roll pattern to play an entire song. The following variation demonstrates using the backward roll (M I T M I T M I) as the primary roll:

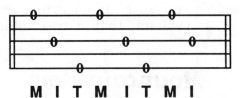

M I T M I T M I

Bile Dem Cabbage Down
(The Backward Roll)

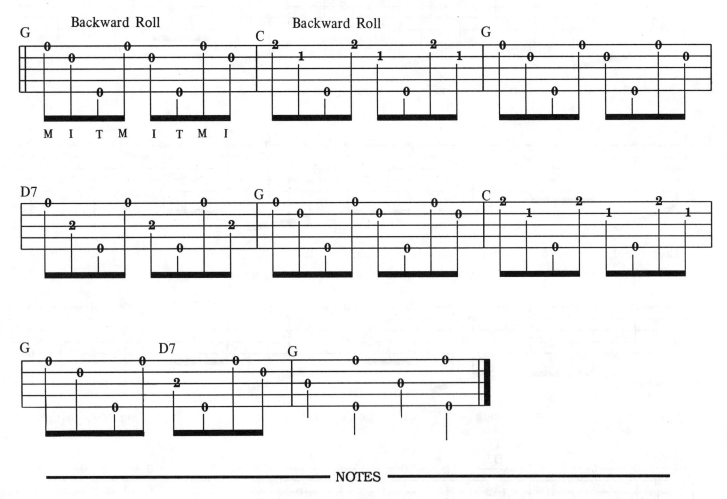

───────── NOTES ─────────

1. For a longer arrangement, play through the tune once using the forward roll, and then play it using the backward roll.

2. For practice, try playing the same chords using the mixed-roll pattern. This would provide another variation.

Lesson 10: The Mixed Roll

• The mixed-roll pattern is played for *each measure* of this tune.

• The right thumb picks the melody notes, and the other two fingers play the background, or harmony notes, based upon the chords of the song.

• Hold the proper chords when indicated. The *D7 chord* is played in the fourth measure. The *C chord* in this tune is played at the 5th fret. This is another position for the C chord:

Barre your index finger across the first three strings at the 5th fret .

Good Night Ladies
(Using the Mixed-Roll Pattern)

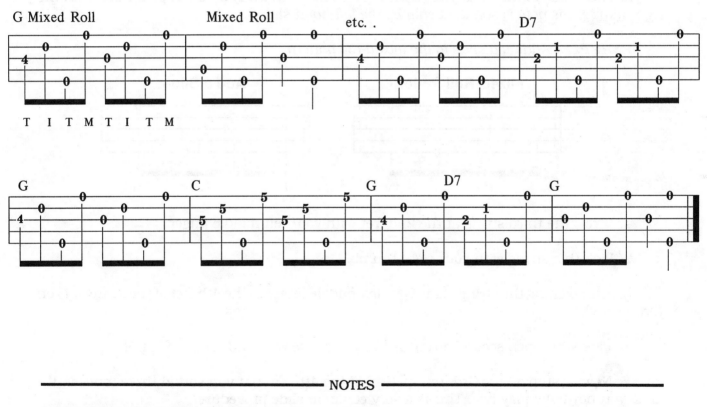

NOTES
---

1. Emphasize the thumb when playing the mixed roll.

2. The thumb picks the melody notes for the mixed roll and for the forward-reverse roll.

Mixed Roll

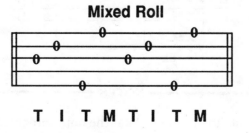

T I T M T I T M

Lesson 11: Left-Hand Techniques

The Slide

Left-hand techniques are often added to a roll pattern to add embellishment to an arrangement. These involve sounding a note with the *left* fingers, rather than picking the string with the right hand. These really contribute to the complete "bluegrass sound." The **slide** is one of the most common of these techniques (indicated SL in the tablature).

"Slide" means that a tone is sounded by the left hand, simply by sliding to the tone. This note has an "SL" written under it in the tablature.

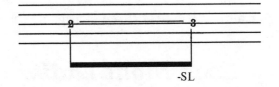

1. Pick the note in front of the slide (2).

2. Then slide to the next note (3 with the SL beneath it). You do not pick the 3 with the right hand. *This note is sounded only by the left-hand slide.*

EXAMPLE: *Adding a slide to the mixed-roll pattern*

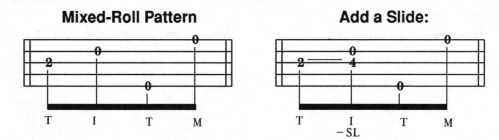

Mixed-Roll Pattern	Add a Slide:

1. "Fret" the third string at the 2nd fret with your left middle finger.

2. Pick this string with your right thumb.

3. After picking the string, slide your left middle finger to the 4th fret of the string it is on (3rd string).

4. Pick your open second string at the *same time* you land on the 4th fret.

5. Now — stop on the 3rd fret, instead of the 4th, so that you sound three tones in the time you normally play two. This is a very common slide procedure:

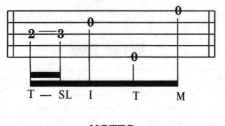

NOTES

It is important to realize, when sliding to a note, that the note you are sliding <u>from</u> is one note, and the note you are sliding <u>to</u> is a different note. Both tones should be sounded . . . the first by picking it, the second by sliding to it.

The following arrangement is just like the arrangement played previously using the mixed-roll pattern (T I T M, etc.). However, it incorporates the slide into this roll pattern. Notice that the song sounds a little more polished, just with this one enhancement.

Good Night Ladies
(Using the Slide)

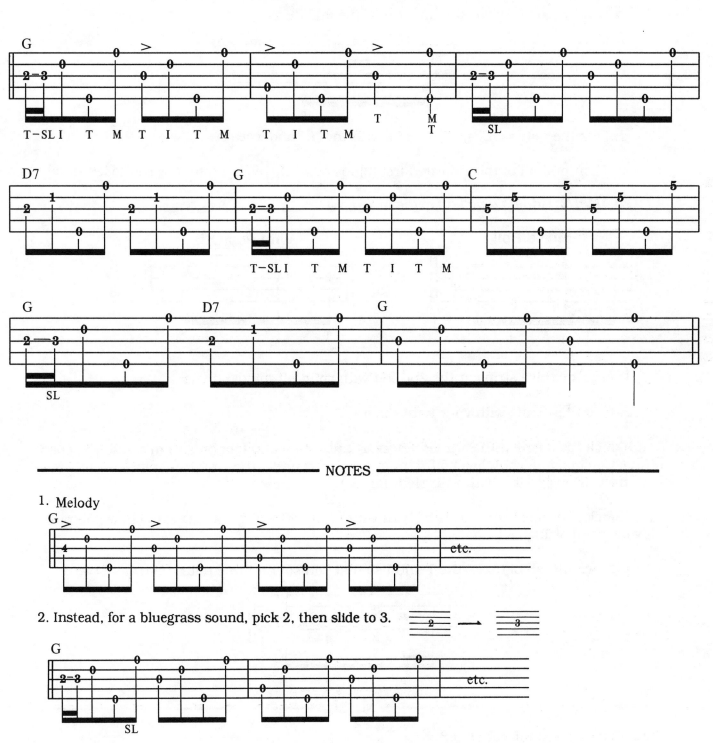

NOTES

1. Melody

2. Instead, for a bluegrass sound, pick 2, then slide to 3.

3. For fun, try to include a slide in "The Gray Goose" and other tunes you have learned.

4. > means to emphasize; e.g. the thumb is emphasized in this tune.

Lesson 12: The Pull-Off

This is one of the most difficult and one of the most exciting of the techniques used to play the banjo. It really adds polish to an arrangement, and helps give it that "bluegrass sound." Remember, the same techniques are used in many different songs, so this is an important one to work with.

Pull-off *(or "push-off") means that a tone is sounded with the left hand* by plucking the string with the left finger, after the string has been sounded by the right hand. You can either pull-off of the string or push the string.

This note has a "P" written under it in the tablature:

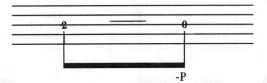

1. Pick the note just *before* the one with the "P" underneath.

2. Then pull-off of the indicated fret (2) to sound the open (0) tone with the left hand.

EXAMPLE: *Adding a pull-off to the mixed roll*

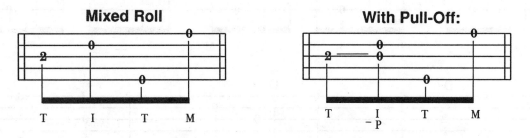

1. Fret the third string at the 2nd fret with your left middle finger.

2. Pick this string with your right *thumb.*

3. Pick the string with your *left finger* by pulling-off of it (popping it) to sound the open string. Don't just lift your finger off of the string . . . get under the string and pluck it with your left finger. (Don't pick it with your right finger.)

4. Pick your open second string with your right index finger at the same time you pull-off your third string.

5. Now, pull-off between the T and I so that you sound three notes instead of two.

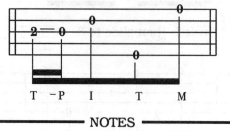

NOTES

In your playing, you will encounter:
   a) pulling-off and picking simultaneously, as in Ex. 1 above, and
   b) pulling-off between two notes, as in the last example.

Lesson 13: The Hammer

This is the only other left-hand technique you will need for a while. *The hammer, the slide, and the pull-off* are the primary left-hand techniques used to play the banjo.

The **hammer** is indicated by an "H" under the note in the tablature.

"Hammer" means that a tone is sounded by "hammering-on" the note with the left finger.

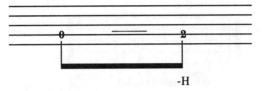

1. First, pick the open fourth string.

2. Then hammer-on the string with the left middle finger at the 2nd fret. (Hit the string at the 2nd fret with the left middle finger to sound the note — then hold it.)

EXAMPLE: *Adding the hammer to the mixed roll*

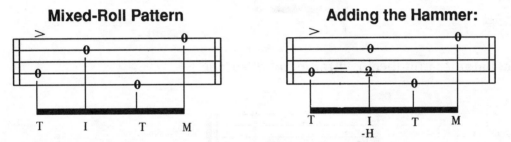

Mixed-Roll Pattern   **Adding the Hammer:**

Remember: You are sounding two tones — the tone before the hammer, and the tone you sound with the left-hand hammer.

1. Pick the fourth string — open.

2. Hit (hammer-on) the 2nd fret with your left middle finger to sound this note (on 2nd fret). Hold this position to let the tone ring.

3. Pick the open second string at the same time you hammer-on the fourth string.

4. Next, hammer between when the thumb and index finger pick the strings in the roll pattern, to sound three tones instead of two.

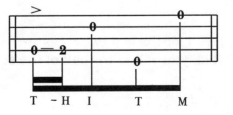

Lesson 14: Cripple Creek

The song "Cripple Creek" is a very popular banjo tune that most three-finger pickers know. The primary roll pattern used for this tune is the *mixed roll*. It is best to learn this song by sections, for this will make it easy to play and easy to remember without your music. First, work on each of the following:

1. The slide unit:

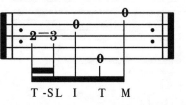

2. The pull-off unit:

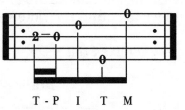

3. The hammer unit (begin with the *fourth string)*:

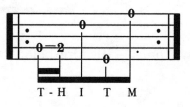

4. Combine the above:

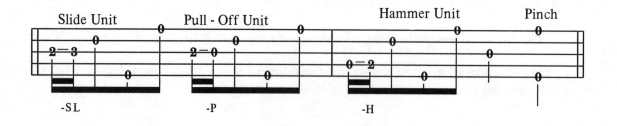

Notice that #4 above is played for the last two measures of each line in "Cripple Creek." When you know how to play this, you will know half of the song.

5. Now, learn Part B of the song (before you learn Part A). (This can also be played as an introduction to begin the song.)

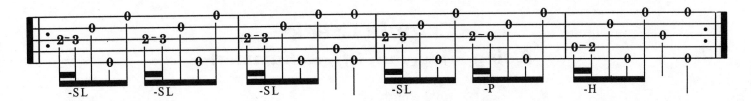

a) Play three slide units in a row.
b) Then play a slide unit, pull-off unit, hammer unit, and end with an open third string and a pinch. (Pinch: Pick the first and fifth strings at the same time.)

6. Now, learn Part A:

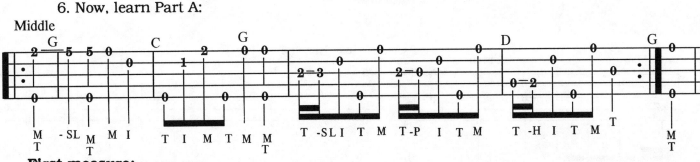

First measure:

a) Notice that it begins with a pinch, and then a slide to the 5th fret. Use your left middle finger on the first string. Pick the pinch, then slide to the 5th fret. *(Do not pick the note with the "SL" under it; it is sounded only by the slide.)*
b) Leave your finger on the 5th fret, and pinch the first and fifth strings again.
c) Pick the open first string (with middle finger).
d) Then, pick the open second string (with index finger). Notice that these are each quarter notes. These are each held evenly and are held twice as long as the eighth notes,(beginning with the C chord.)

Second measure:

a) Hold a C chord with the left hand first. Then play the notes (partial forward roll). These are played twice as fast as the notes in the first measure.
b) Release the C chord, play the first string, then pinch. (This is like punctuation for a sentence.)

Third and fourth measures:

See Step 4 above to finish Part A.

Note: *Do not pause between the units — only pause after a quarter note (e.g. pinch).*

Now you should be able to play the entire arrangement below. Part A is written out completely; Part B uses a repeat sign — so play it twice.

Cripple Creek
(Using Slide, Pull-Off, & Hammer)

Lesson 15: Melodic Style

It is often fun to play two different arrangements of the same tune. The following arrangement introduces a new style of playing called *melodic style* or *fiddle style.* In melodic style, the left hand holds positions from a scale rather than chord positions.

Notice in this arrangement that the *right hand* is playing a roll pattern for every measure. *Which roll pattern is it?**

Cripple Creek
(Melodic Style)

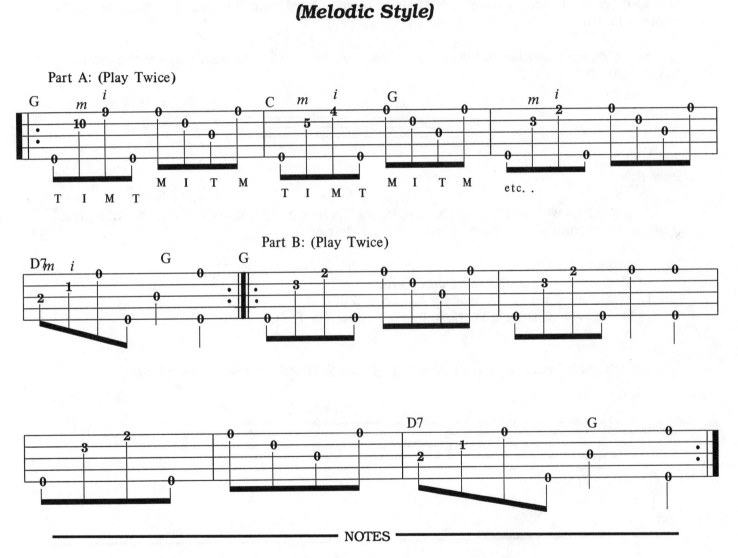

Part A: (Play Twice)

Part B: (Play Twice)

NOTES

---

1. Play Part A twice; then play Part B twice. (Many fiddle tunes use this form.)

2. Left-hand fingers appear *above* the tablature *(m i).*

*Answer: The forward-reverse roll. (We will be concerned with the actual scales later on.)

A NOTE OF ENCOURAGEMENT

It is important to keep in mind that learning to play the banjo is a building process . . . each new technique you learn will be used in almost every song you play in the future. The things that seem difficult now will be like old friends when you run across them in new songs.

Lesson 16: Blackberry Blossom

This is a fiddle tune which is popular among both banjo players and fiddle players. It is divided into two parts, which is a common feature of many fiddle tunes. *Learn each part separately (as you did with "Cripple Creek"), then put it together.*

Part A:

• Notice that each measure of Part A plays the *forward-reverse roll* (T I M T M I T M).

• *Each measure (roll) contains two different chords* (involving two left-hand positions). The first four notes of each measure (roll) belong to one chord, and the last four notes belong to another chord.

• Use the left index (or middle) finger to *barre* across the first three strings at the indicated fret for Part A:

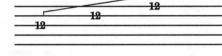

Part B:

• This begins with an *E-minor chord position.* It is held exactly like the C chord, but without fretting the second string. (The second string is left open.)

• Notice in Part B:
a) Measures 1, 3, and 5 are exactly alike.
b) Measures 1 and 2 are exactly like mm. 5 and 6.
c) Measure 4 calls for a B chord (barre across 4th fret).

EXERCISE: *Pinch the first three strings for each chord, and play with rhythm:*

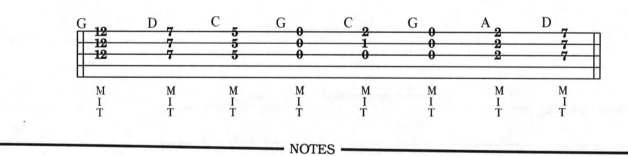

——————— NOTES ———————

1. There are only three left-hand chord patterns for the major chords. The barre position is one of these.

2. Any chord can be played with the barre position: G is open; A = 2nd fret; B = 4th fret; C = 5th fret; D = 7th fret; E = 9th fret; F = 10th fret; G = 12th fret.

Barre Position

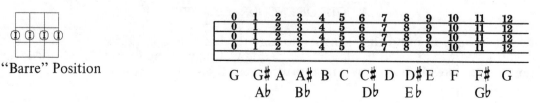

"Barre" Position

Use the forward-reverse roll with the right hand for Part A. Use the barre-chord position with the left hand. Play Part A twice; then play Part B twice.

Blackberry Blossom

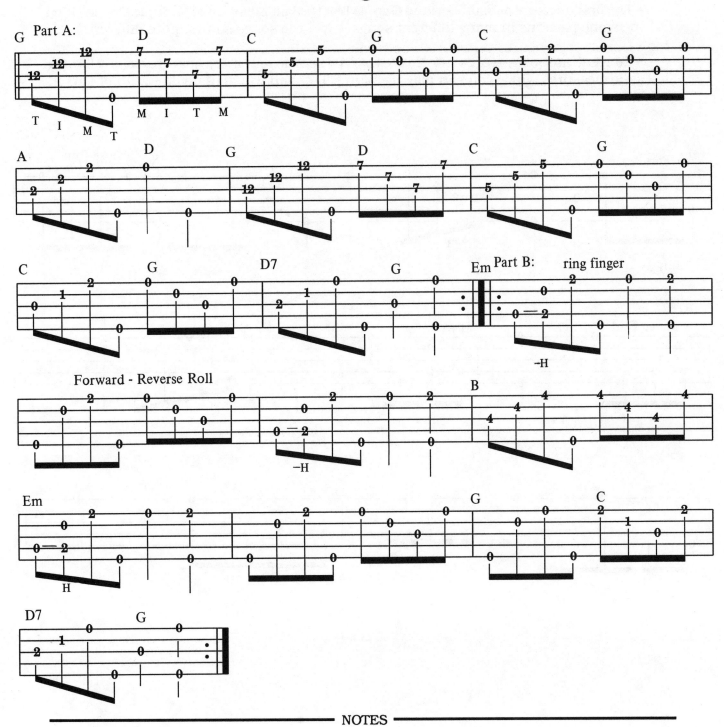

Forward - Reverse Roll

NOTES
---

1. Do not stop between each roll; change chords quickly with the left hand. Don't lift your left finger — slide it to get to the next chord. Even if you don't get there in time, keep the right hand "rolling"!

2. Part B introduces the B chord (barre 4th fret).

3. Part B also introduces the E-minor chord position.

Lesson 17: Cumberland Gap

This tune is divided into three sections. Each section is a variation of "Cumberland Gap" and can be played separately. However, it is customary to play them as one break. Learn this tune a section at a time (Lesson 17 through Lesson 19).

Part A:

• The first measure of "Cumberland Gap" is like the last measure of "Cripple Creek." (You use the same patterns in many different songs — yet the songs sound quite different.)

• Concentrate on measures 1–4. Notice that the second four measures are exactly like the first four measures. Once you can play measures 1–4, you will actually know all of Part A.

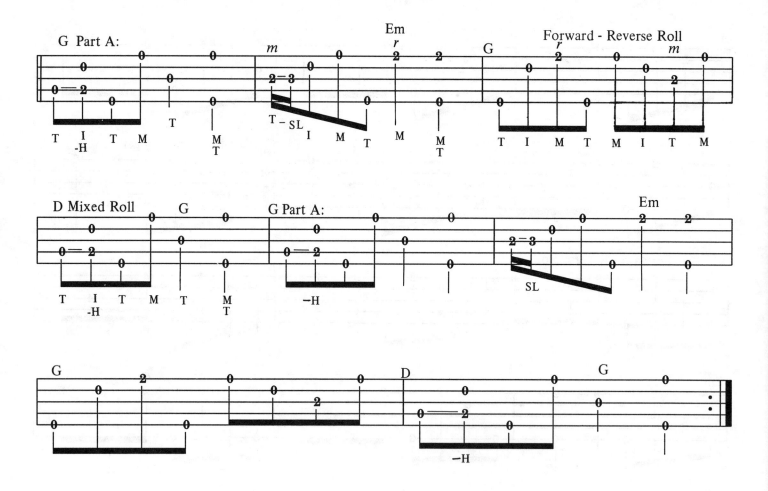

Lesson 18: Playing Up the Neck

"Cumberland Gap" — Part B

After you know how to play the previous variation well, begin Part B. This variation is played up the neck, using the higher fret numbers of the fingerboard. This area of the fingerboard is always referred to as **up the neck.**

Part B:

• The left hand holds the same chord position throughout this entire part. Notice the left-hand fingering!

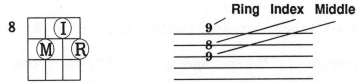

• Your pinky finger will fret the 11th fret each time it occurs in the song. Keep holding the chord position with the other fingers.

This pattern is used in just about every up-the-neck arrangement. **Keep on trying — you will eventually get it!** It is true. Even if your little finger doesn't work at all, it will learn. It may be unnatural at first, but it will become easier and easier.

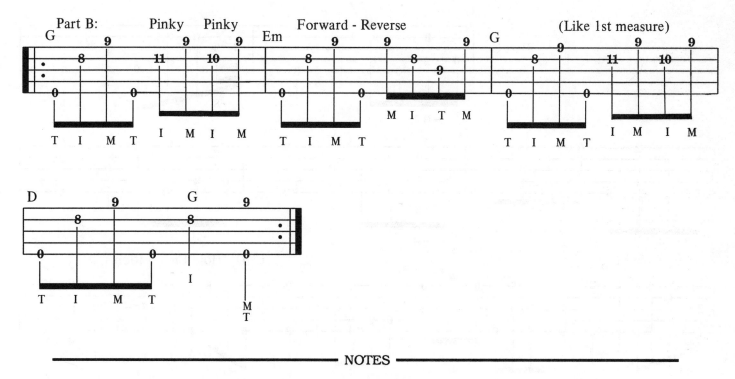

NOTES

After you learn this part, play it with your right hand closer to the fingerboard — away from the bridge. This is the right-hand position when playing up the neck.

Lesson 19 : Adding an Ending

"Cumberland Gap" — Part C

Part C:

This part is exactly like Part A. Now you know the entire song. Add an ending to make it complete.

The Ending:

• Consists of the last two measures of the song.

• The left hand holds the same chord position you used to play Part B.

• At the end of measure 1 of the end, move your middle finger "down" to the 7th fret, then pick this note.

• Then — slide your middle finger "up" to about the 12th fret. You should hear the slide — this is a technique.

• Then pick the last two notes!

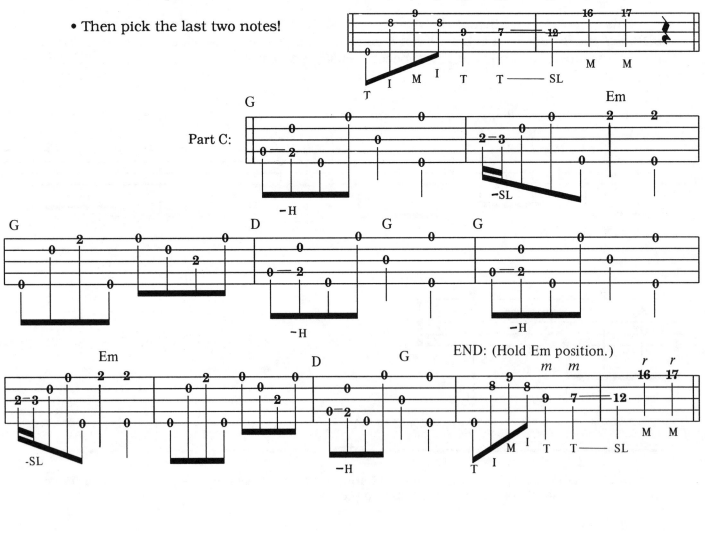

NOTES

This ending can be tacked onto the end of any song. Try it with "Cripple Creek."

Cumberland Gap
(Complete)

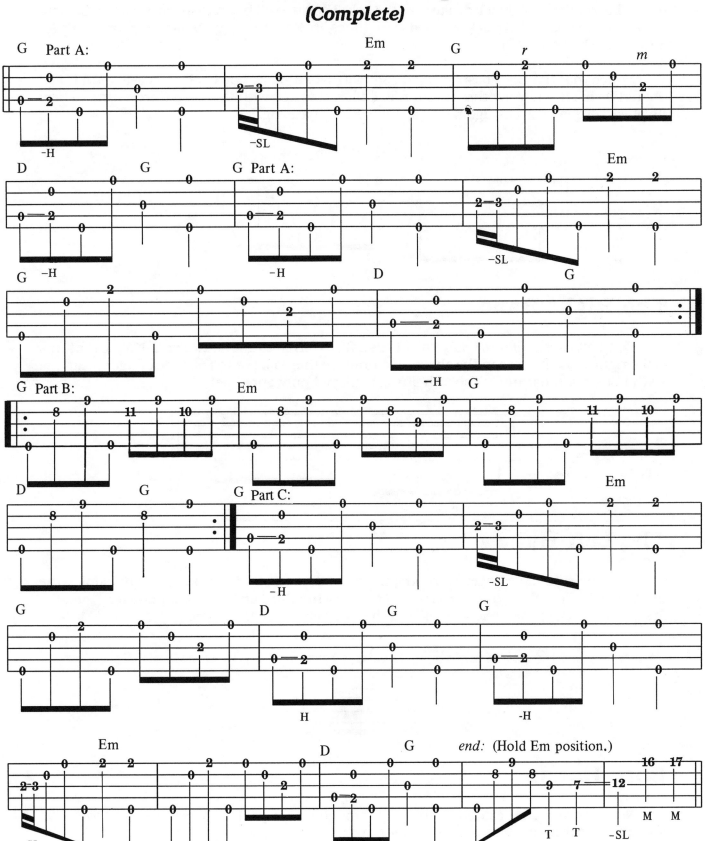

Lesson 20: The G Lick

Now it is time to learn a **lick.** A lick is like a roll pattern, but it is used only for one chord. Actually, a lick *is* a roll pattern, but it includes hammers or slides, etc., and can only be used for a specific chord.

The following is a *G-chord lick.* This lick is used at least once in virtually every song played on the banjo. For now, just learn to play the lick. Then we will begin to insert it for the G chord in different songs. (This lick is used four times in Earl Scruggs' basic version of "Foggy Mountain Breakdown.")

Notice that the lick doesn't sound complete when played by itself. A lick is a unit, and should be followed by another lick or roll. Follow this lick with the open third string to hear its effect, or play the lick again and again without pausing.

The G Lick

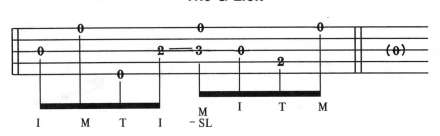

The Right Hand

This lick uses a *fifth-roll pattern.* It is usually referred to as the **tag roll.** Notice that this is the right-hand pattern in the above lick. Practice this roll. **Hint:** The index finger picks the sixth note, *not* the thumb. The fifth string is played only one time!

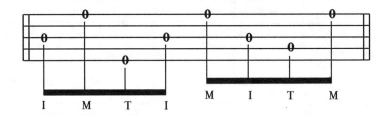

The Left Hand

Use the left middle finger to fret the third string at the 2nd fret. Pick this note (pick the third string). Now slide to the 3rd fret (do not pick the third string again, however). Pick the first string at the same time you slide to the 3rd fret on the third string.

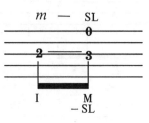

Both Hands

Now return to the lick above, and play through it slowly. Then play it over and over, like an exercise, without a break in your rhythm.

The G lick is often used for the final G chord of a song. Notice how it adds punctuation, or a sense of finality to the break.

Bile Dem Cabbage Down
(Using the G Lick)

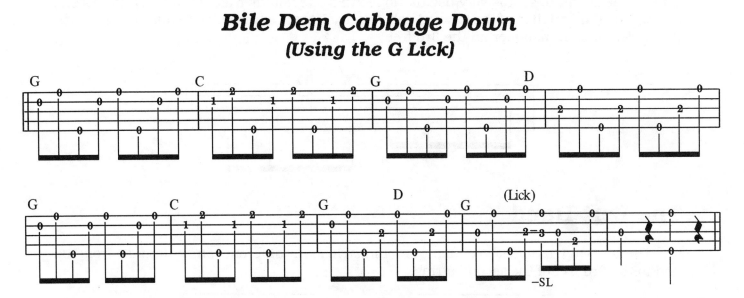

The G lick is also effective when used in a song to fill in the pause at the end of a phrase — again serving as punctuation for the music. (Licks used in this manner are often referred to as *fill-in licks.*)

Wildwood Flower
(Using the G Lick)

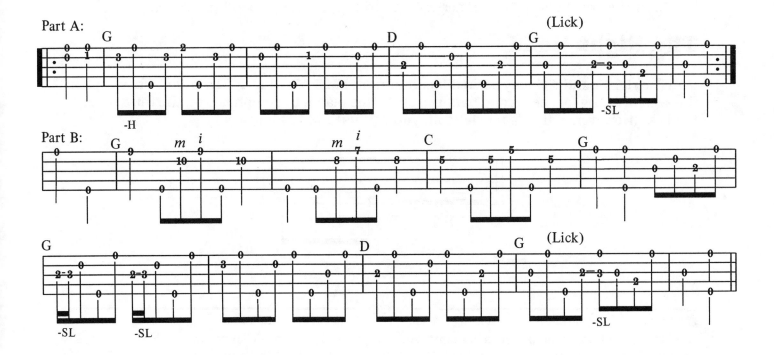

Lesson 21: G Lick #2

The Foggy Mountain Lick

This lick is used to begin many bluegrass breakdowns. It can be used for both the G chord and for the D chord, so it is very useful. Notice that the hammer technique is used twice in a row. This is a variation of the forward-roll pattern. **Note:** Leave your left index finger on the 2nd fret when you hammer on the 3rd fret.

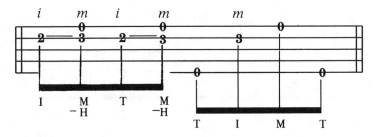

The Left Hand

The following "hammer" technique is common in many different songs. Hammer from the 2nd to the 3rd fret of the second string.

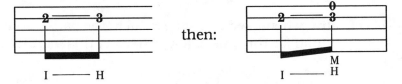

1. Fret the 2, and pick the second string. (Use the index finger with each hand.)

2. Hammer-on the 3rd fret with the left middle finger. Do not pick the second string here — this note is sounded by hammering only.

3. At the *same time* you hammer-on the 3rd fret, pick the open first string.

The Right Hand

The right-hand roll may seem difficult at first: I M T M T I M T. The *thumb* should pick the second string for the second hammer unit. This places the emphasis on the third note in the lick. (However, if this is too difficult, you can use I M I M for now.)

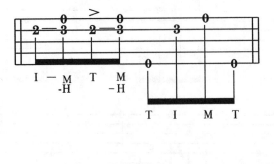

───────────────── NOTES ─────────────────

Any time a G-chord symbol occurs in a song, you can play either of the G licks you have learned. These are interchangeable because they work for the same chord. These will work in almost any song, as long as they are played for the G chord.

- Notice that G Lick #2 is played three times in a row at the beginning (first three measures).

- Notice that this arrangement ends with the G Lick #1 from Lesson 20.

- Notice the repeat sign (:‖). Play through this variation twice.

Train 45
(Variation I)

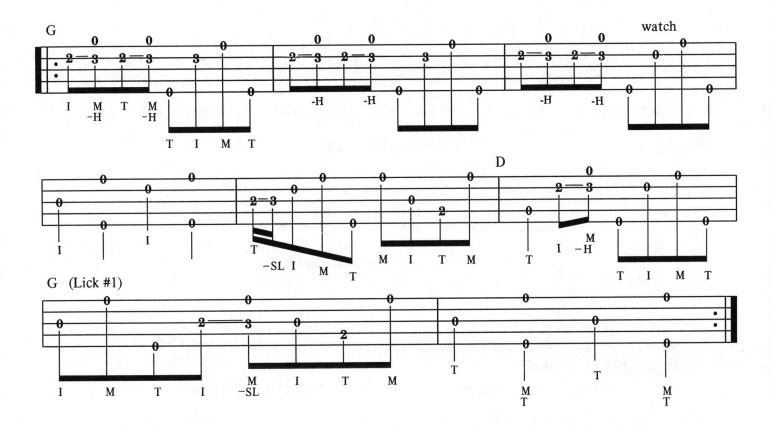

Lesson 22: G Lick #3

Pull-Off Lick

Another common technique is to pull-off of a string from one fret to a lower fret number, e.g.: 3–2.

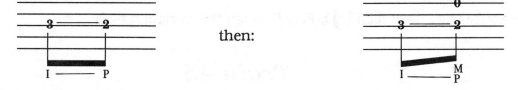

then:

1. Place your left middle finger on the 3rd fret (third string). Also: put your index finger on the 2nd fret, third string (at the same time).

2. Pick the third string.

3. Pull-off or push off of (pluck) the 3rd fret with your left middle finger. *Leave your index finger on the 2nd fret!!!* Do not pick the string again — the note is sounded by the left hand.

4. Pick the open first string at the same time you pull-off the third string, 3rd fret.

Lick Using the P

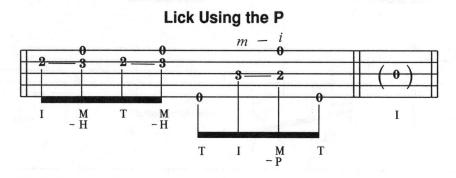

Notice that the roll pattern is like the Foggy Mountain lick, but it includes the pull-off with the left hand, and it also picks the third string. (Play both licks with the right hand only, using open strings to compare.)

Foggy "Roll" Pattern   ### Pull-Off Roll Pattern

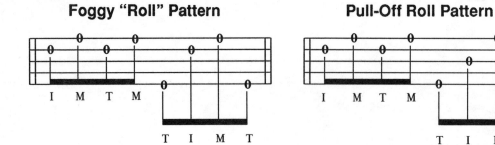

Substitute Lick #3 using the pull-off. Find this lick each time it occurs before playing the song.

Train 45
(Variation II)

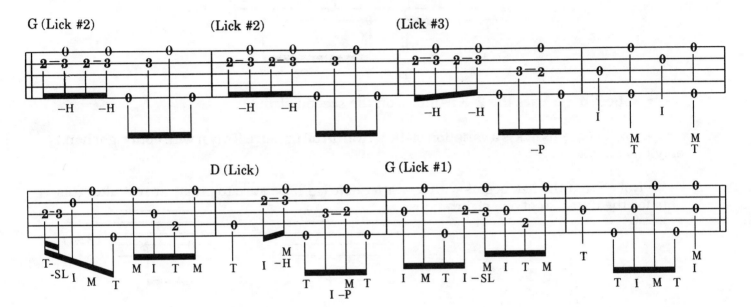

Lesson 23: D Lick #1

The Salty Dog Lick

The following pattern can be played when a *D chord* occurs in a song. Therefore, this is a D lick.

Salty Dog D Lick

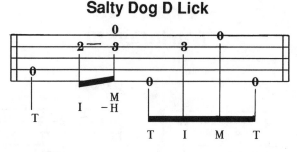

• Notice that it uses the 2–3 hammer on the second string.

   • Notice that this lick is a variation of the forward-roll pattern. (Play it with your right hand only.)

   • Notice that the lick begins with a *quarter note* (♩). Be sure to *pause* or rest after this note for the duration of one eighth note:

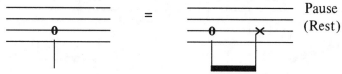

This lick will be used for the D chord at the end of many different songs. (Yes, many songs end alike.) The following arrangement of "Salty Dog" uses the above lick for the first measure of the D chord; the second measure of the D chord uses the Foggy Lick (#2). (Remember, this lick can be used for both the G chord and the D chord.*)

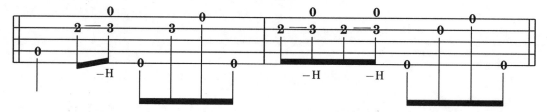

When combined, these two licks create *one D lick (2 mm.)* which is often used for the final D chord in a song, just before the standard G lick.

The G Lick #3 can also be played for the second measure, for the D chord. (Yes, this means that G #3 can also be used as a D lick.*)

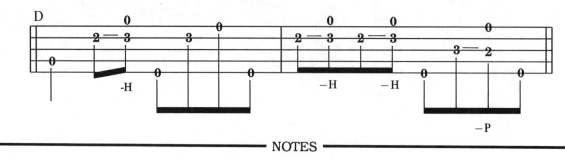

─────────────── NOTES ───────────────

*The D tone (open first and fourth strings) belongs to the G chord and the D chord; therefore, many licks using these strings can be played for either chord.

Sunnyvale Breakdown
(Using Licks G #1, G #2, G #3, D #1)

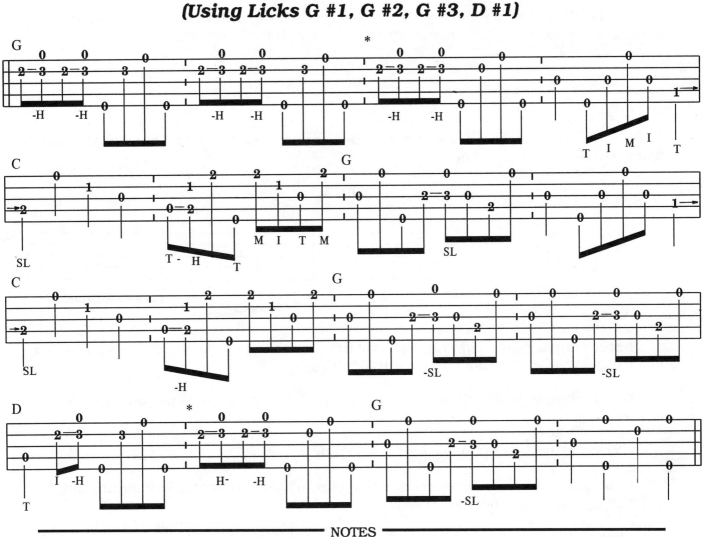

NOTES

*1. For a showier effect: substitute G #3 for the second measure of D #1 and for the third measure, first line.

2. Although the above song begins with the same lick used for "Train 45," the two songs sound completely different.

3. To move to the C chord: Pick the 1 on the fourth string — then *slide* to the 2nd fret, e.g.:

4. Notice also that this is a partial C chord — the first string is left open for color or tension.

5. If you want to play "Foggy Mountain Breakdown," simply substitute an E-minor chord where the C-chord measures occur. You can play the same right-hand roll patterns for the E-minor measures, or you can vary them. (Omit your index finger from the C-chord position to form an E-minor chord:

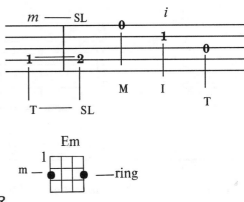

A SUMMARY . . . SO FAR

As you gain experience by playing several different songs on the banjo, you will begin to find similarities among all of the songs. So far, we have discovered the fact that different songs can use the same roll patterns and licks, and they may also use the same chords.

Lesson 25: D Lick #2

Partial D Chord

Most of the songs you will play on the banjo will involve the D chord. Until now, we have worked only with the D7 position: **D7** and with the Salty Dog D lick.

It is also very common to use a partial D-chord position, by fretting only the third and fourth strings to play the chord:

Partial D

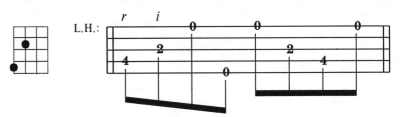

Note: Normally, your left *ring finger* will fret the 4th fret on the fourth string. Your left *index finger* will fret the 2nd fret on the third string.

Before playing through "Wabash Cannonball," look for the patterns you have already learned:

• Note the use of the "Cripple Creek" slide unit.

• Notice the C chord when it occurs. Remember to hold the chord before starting into the roll with the right hand (forward-reverse).

• Notice the roll pattern in measure 8 (the tag roll). You can also substitute the G lick here.

• Notice the lick in the third from the last measure. (This is a new ending D lick.) Notice the right hand is playing the *mixed roll pattern:* (T I T M - T I T M).

D Lick #2

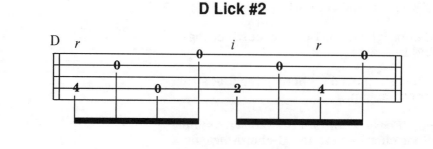

—————————————————————— NOTES ——————————————————————

The full D-chord position uses all four strings:

This will also be used in songs later on.

46

Wabash Cannonball

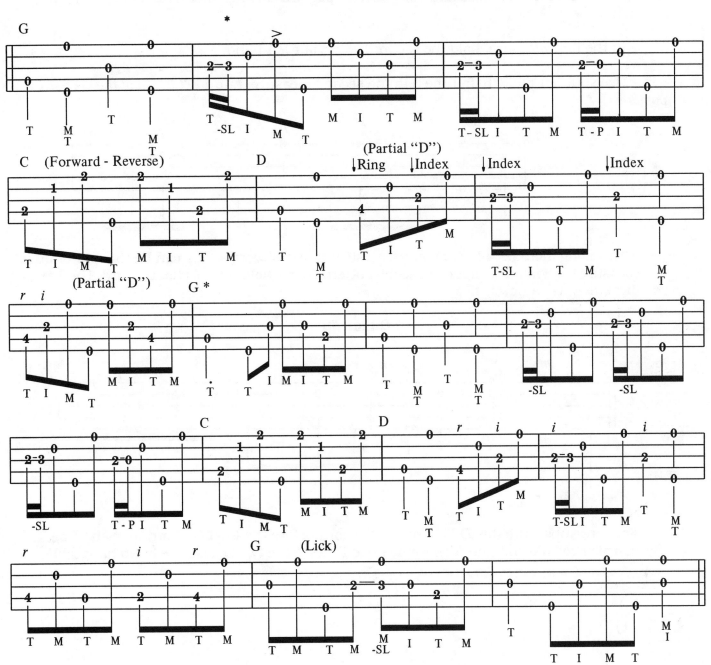

*For fun:

1. Substitute this for the second measure: (There are many possible ideas for playing any song.)

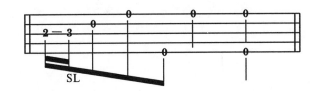

2. Substitute this for the eighth measure:

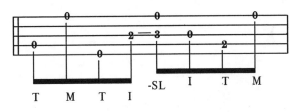

47

Lesson 26: D Lick #3

"John Hardy" is a very popular bluegrass song and can be a lot of fun to play. You should recognize most of the patterns and licks used to play this arrangement. As usual, there are a couple of new items:

- In the first measure, hold the C chord with your left hand.

- Use your left pinky to fret the 3 in the second measure, but *don't let go of the C-chord position.*

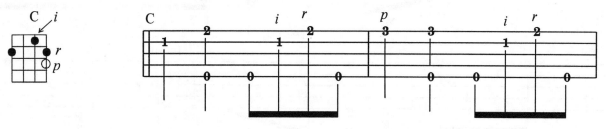

- This song includes a long *D chord* . . . six measures' worth. This can be thought of in two-measure sections: The first two use roll patterns while holding a partial D chord. The last two measures use a new D lick.

D Lick #3

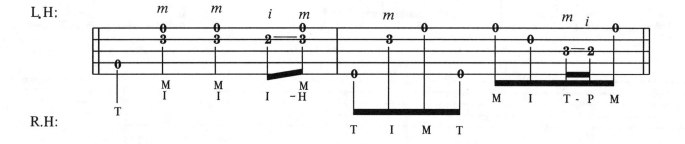

For fun, substitute this D lick for the D chord before the final G chord in "Salty Dog," "Sunnyvale Breakdown," and "Lonesome Road Blues." The two D licks are interchangeable.

John Hardy

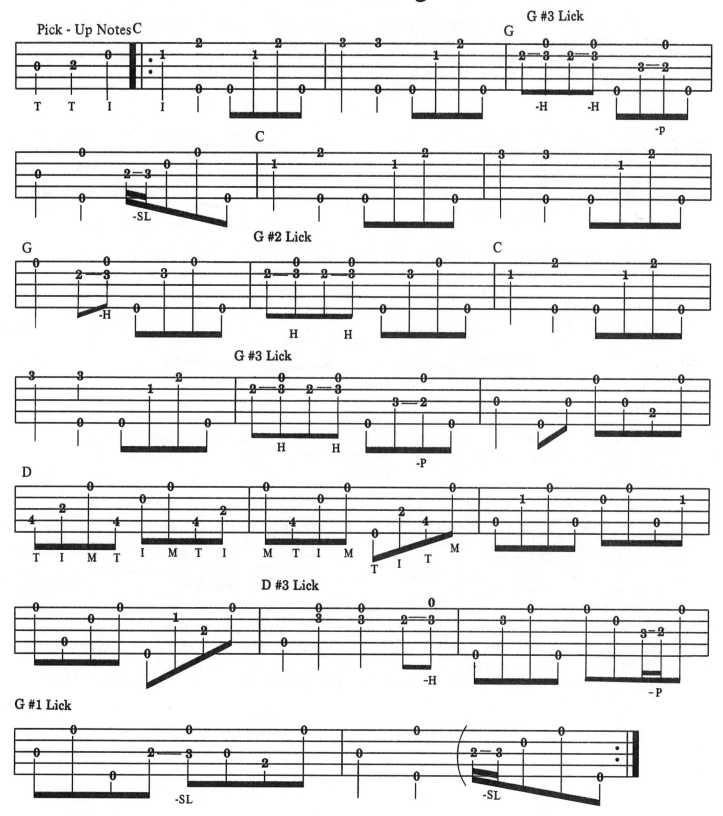

Lesson 27:
Using Alternate Licks

The variation of "John Hardy" on the following page demonstrates how licks can be interchanged to play the same song. The key, as you now know, is to substitute licks according to the chord for which they are played . . . and, of course, for the same number of measures, e.g. compare the third measure in each arrangement. These licks are interchangeable for the G chord in *any* song.

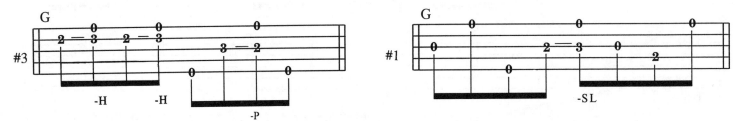

Also, the long (six-measure) D chord works with a two-measure pattern:

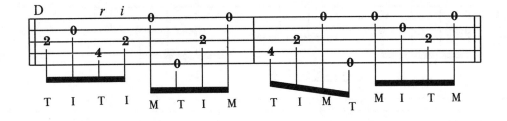

Compare the last two measures of the D chord with the last two measure of the D chord in the first arrangement. As we noted previously, these licks are interchangeable for the D chord.

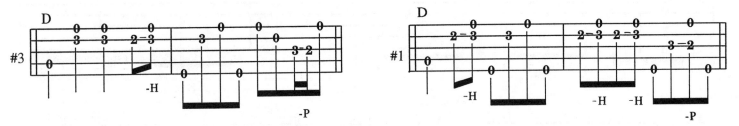

This arrangement should be easier to play than the first arrangement, simply because you have already worked with these licks, and they are familiar to you. Choose the easiest combination of licks for you at this time, but keep working on all of the licks, for eventually they will also become like old friends. (Eventually, you will naturally use these without thinking.)

John Hardy
(Using Different Licks)

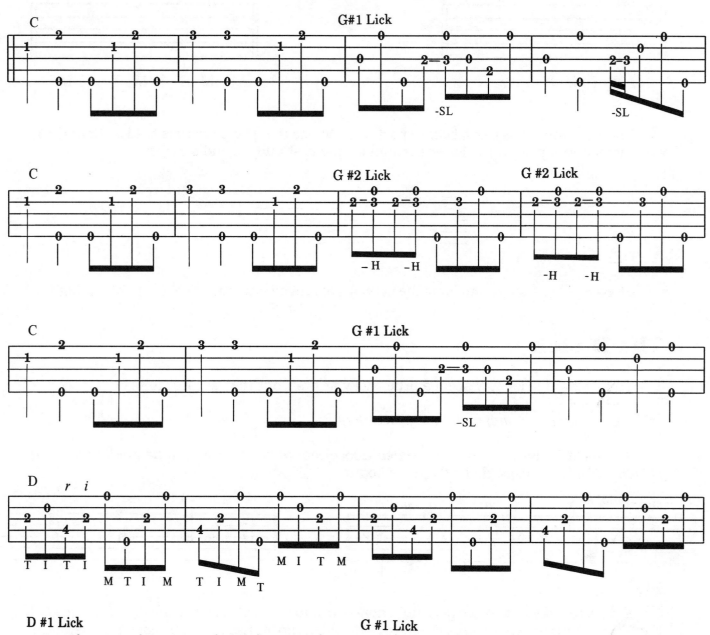

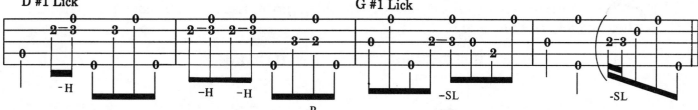

Lesson 28: Up the Neck

The higher fret numbers should not seem so ominous once you realize that you are playing patterns here, also. The following arrangement of "John Hardy" uses *the Foggy Mountain roll pattern plus the forward roll as a two-measure pattern:*

The left hand holds partial chord positions. Notice that the C chord is held at 13 and 14, exactly as it was held in the lower position on the first and second strings:

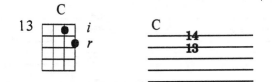

Therefore, this is very similar to the previous arrangement, but it is played 12 frets higher.

The D Lick

The D-chord licks may seem a little tricky at first, but they are fun to play.

• *Use your left thumb to fret the fifth string!*

• *The left-hand fingering is indicated above the tablature. You will be holding a chord position which will move down the fingerboard:*

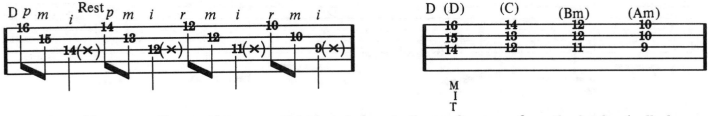

• Also, remember to place your right hand close to the neck, away from the bridge (called the "Y position") when playing up the neck. Remember, "up the neck" means moving to the higher pitches (higher fret numbers).

Full C Chord

(Hold all four strings.)

Full D Chord

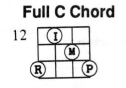

(All four strings.)

John Hardy
(Up-the-Neck Arrangement)

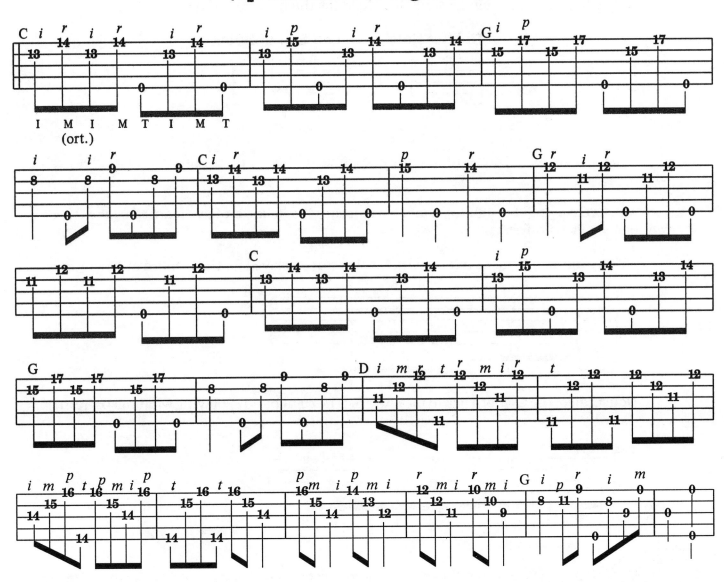

Tag Ending:

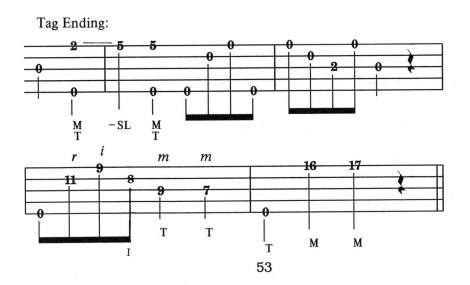

Lesson 29: Quarter Notes

Although the basic roll patterns consist of eight eighth notes, songs also often include quarter notes. This is quite simple to understand....

A quarter note has a single stem. It is held for the duration of two eighth notes.

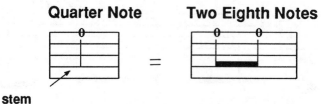

• "Lonesome Road Blues" uses quite a few quarter notes. Be careful to pause after each one.

• Before playing through the song, try to locate the licks you have learned so far. These will now be like old friends.

• This tune *also includes a C-chord lick* which can be played for the C chord in other tunes.

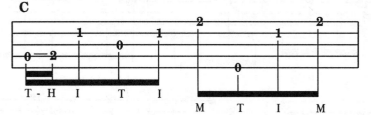

Notice, also, the G-chord lick in measure 3. (The right hand is playing what roll pattern?)*

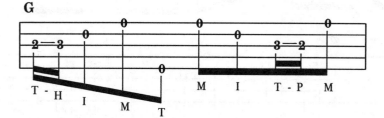

This song uses exactly the same chord progression used to play "Sunny Valley Breakdown" . . . but the tunes sound completely different. Why?**

NOTES

*The forward-reverse roll pattern.
**They have different melodies and use different licks.

Lonesome Road Blues

NOTES

> means to emphasize or accent this note (melody note).

Lesson 30: G Lick #4

This tune will give you the opportunity to practice what you have learned so far. Before you begin, look over the tablature and find:

- The "Cripple Creek" slide unit.

- The basic G Lick #1.

I might also mention that left-hand techniques can also be used to start a lick:

- The first measure begins with a slide (forward roll).

- The sixth measure begins with a pull-off.

Isolate these measures, and practice them over and over — make an exercise of them.

G Lick #4

(This lick occurs at the end of the variation. It is commonly interchanged with G #1.)

This tune also includes a special half measure (see m. 8). You will come across this from time to time in other bluegrass tunes. Actually, it should not feel unusual when playing through the song; however, it will help to accent the first note in the measure. (Your guitar player will complain; he may accuse you of playing extra notes if he doesn't know the tune.)

Down the Road

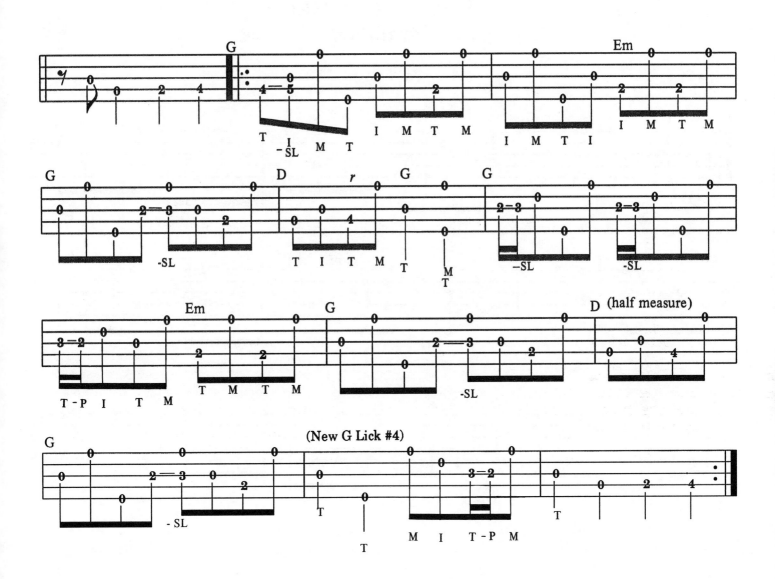

The following arrangement shifts the left-hand techniques to a different area in the measure. These alterations result in different licks that can also be used for the same chord in other songs.

Down the Road
(Variation)

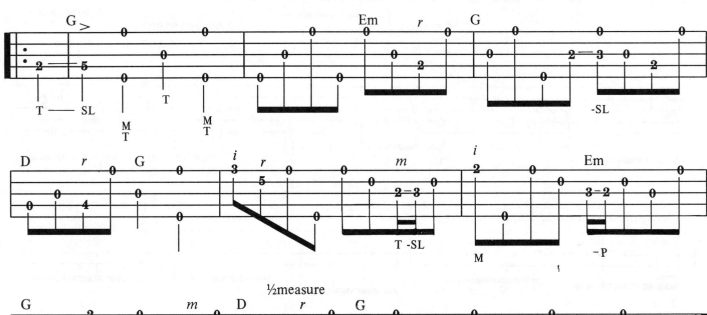

Lesson 31: Pig in a Pen

"Pig in a Pen" is a popular bluegrass song which has been recorded by many different bluegrass bands.

The first arrangement:

• Uses the mixed roll as the primary roll pattern for the G chord, and the forward-roll pattern for the C-chord measures.

  • Should be played twice:
a) Play to the repeat sign the first time: ⌐1.

b) Return to the repeat sign at the beginning ‖: and play through the arrangement again.
c) This time, skip the first ending, and play the second ending instead: ⌐2.
d) The tag ending is optional.

The second and third arrangements are more advanced:*

  • Notice the frequent use of quarter notes for emphasis in the second arrangement.

  • The third arrangement shifts the emphasis to the middle of the first measure, by playing a "pinch."

  • Notice how the rolls and licks in these arrangements differ from the basic rolls used for the first variation.

NOTES

You often have the choice of using a slide or of using a hammer, especially in a 2-3 situation on the third string. However, when numbers go the other way, 3-2, you should always pull or push off. Do not slide backwards.

*"Advanced" does not always mean more difficult to play. In this case it demonstrates advanced licks and rolls, which produce a slightly "different" effect (syncopation).

Pig in a Pen
(Variation I: Using Standard Rolls and Licks)

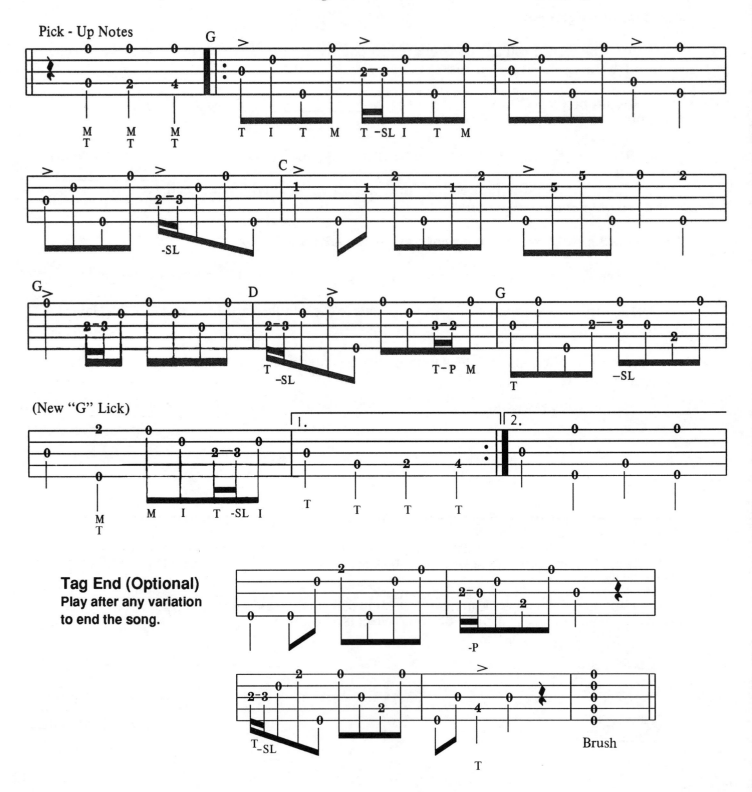

Tag End (Optional)
Play after any variation
to end the song.

Pig in a Pen
(Variation II: Using Quarter Notes for Emphasis)

Pig in a Pen
(Variation III: Varying the Rolls and Licks)

Lesson 32: G Lick #5

"Sally Goodin' " is a very popular fiddle tune that most bluegrass musicians love to play. The following is a common rendition used by many banjo players when it is played in the open-string-to-5th-fret area of the fingerboard. This tune is wide open for variation possibilities.

• Notice that this tune uses the *G chord* for almost every measure.

• Notice that the melody (singable tune) is somewhat vague. This means that you can substitute various G licks and be fairly safe. (Many breakdowns are also of this nature.)

• Notice that this arrangement uses most of the left-hand techniques (slides, hammers, pull-offs) you have already learned. Are you beginning to notice that the hammer often occurs from 2-3 on the second string? And a pull-off is frequent on the third string from 3-2? Also, the slide is often used on the third string from 2-3. These should look fairly familiar to you by now.

• Notice that the measure connecting Part A with Part B is a *half measure*. It adds an extra surge to the music without changing the tempo (speeding it up). Don't stop between the last note of Part A and the first note of Part B.

Note: Some bands omit this measure. If it doesn't fit with your band . . . leave it out.

G Lick #5

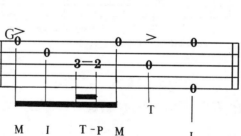

You may see several variations of this lick.

Sally Goodin'

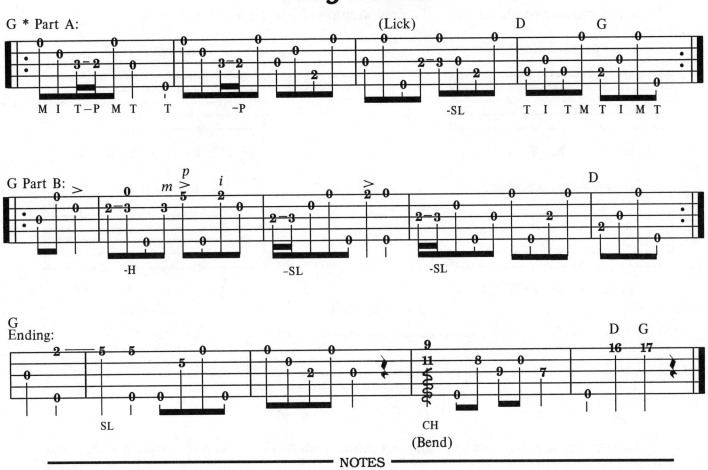

─────────────────────────── NOTES ───────────────────────────

*Notice the *repeat signs.* Play Part A twice, then play Part B twice!

Review

Banjo music usually consists of a combination of the basic roll patterns:

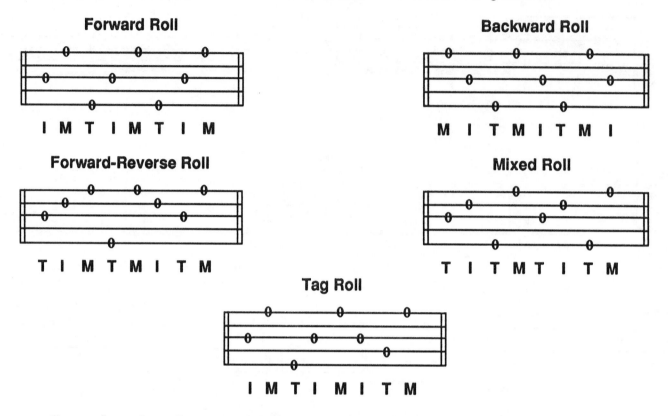

Forward Roll

I M T I M T I M

Backward Roll

M I T M I T M I

Forward-Reverse Roll

T I M T M I T M

Mixed Roll

T I T M T I T M

Tag Roll

I M T I M I T M

Remember, the rolls can use *different* strings; each roll pattern is simply a *right-hand* pattern. The order in which the fingers follow one another when picking the strings determines which roll pattern is being played.

Also, banjo players are free to alter a roll pattern (change the fingering order when the urge arises). This may be done for a variety of reasons. It may be just for the fun of it, or it may be to help the right-hand fingers roll more smoothly into the next measure. Sometimes, the melody notes fit better if you change the fingering order. Sometimes it makes a passage easier to play. However, any measure can usually be identified as belonging to a certain roll pattern. Even the licks you play are each a variation of a specific roll pattern.

For example, the Foggy Mountain lick is a variation of the forward roll:

Move the first two notes to the end of the roll pattern.

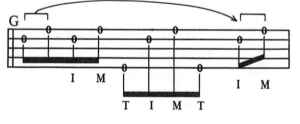

Also, the rolls can be played for any chord.

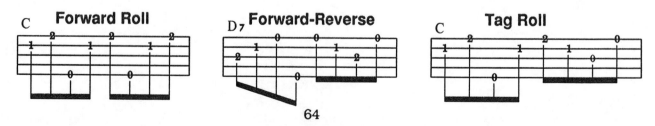

Forward Roll

Forward-Reverse

Tag Roll

Lesson 33: Roll-Pattern Variations

The first few song arrangements in this book demonstrated how to use *the same roll pattern* for every measure in a song. The following arrangement uses a *combination* of rolls, and the fingering patterns often throw in a surprise. This arrangement should be slightly more difficult to play than the earlier ones, but it should also sound more polished.

• Try to identify the "mother roll pattern" when a measure is difficult to play. Hint: Look at the slant of the tablature,

e.g.　　/ / /　　　　　or　　　/ \　　　　　or　　　\ \ \

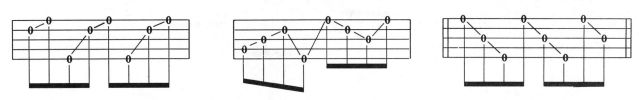

| Forward Roll | Forward-Reverse | Backward Roll |

• In the arrangement of "Coming Around the Mountain" on the following page, notice that the forward roll is the primary roll pattern, but many of the measures change the fingering order or the string order. Each of these rolls is a forward-roll pattern:

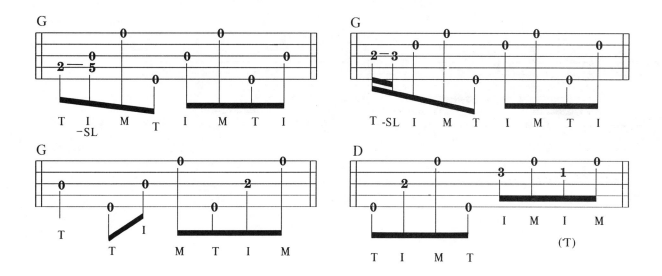

She'll Be Coming Around the Mountain

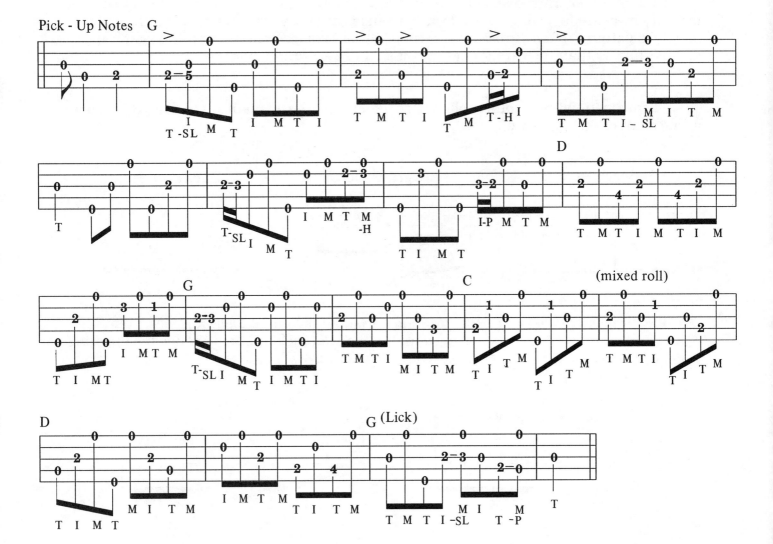

Lesson 34: Harmonics

"Grandfather's Clock" is a traditional tune that has been handed down through many generations. Look over the following arrangement for the items we have learned so far. Which roll pattern is used as the "primary roll pattern"?*

Also, notice the use of the following:

- Pick-up notes
- The forward-reverse roll for the C chord
- The partial D chord
- The basic G Lick #1
- Quarter notes
- How Part A and Part B are connected (pick-up notes)
- Harmonics in Part C

Harmonics

Part C of this song uses a technique called **harmonics** or **chimes,**** which can be a lot of fun to play.

To play harmonics:

1. *Lightly touch the first string* with your left middle finger, *directly over the 12th fret bar.* (Place it directly over the metal bar . . . not between the bars, where you would normally depress the string.) Do not depress the string . . . just touch it.

2. Now, *pick the string* with your right finger or thumb.

3. *Lift your left finger off of the string* so that the tone can ring. This produces the harmonic or chime.

Harmonics can also be produced on the other three strings at the 12th fret. Lightly barre your left middle finger across all four strings at the 12th fret. Pick any or all of the strings, and release your left finger.

Chimes can be played only over certain fret bars: e.g. 12th, 5th, 7th, 19th, 4th. Harmonics play a G chord at the 12th fret and at the 5th fret; a D chord at the 7th fret and at the 19th fret; and a B chord at the 4th fret.

──────────────── NOTES ────────────────

*The forward roll: I M T I M T I M.
**When playing harmonics, you are literally dividing the string in ½ at the 12th fret, in ⅓ at 7th fret, or in ¼ at the 5th fret. Harmonics can also be found over other frets (e.g. the 4th fret), but they are harder to produce clearly.

The last section of this tune plays "harmonics" (in Part C). Watch your timing in this section.

Grandfather's Clock

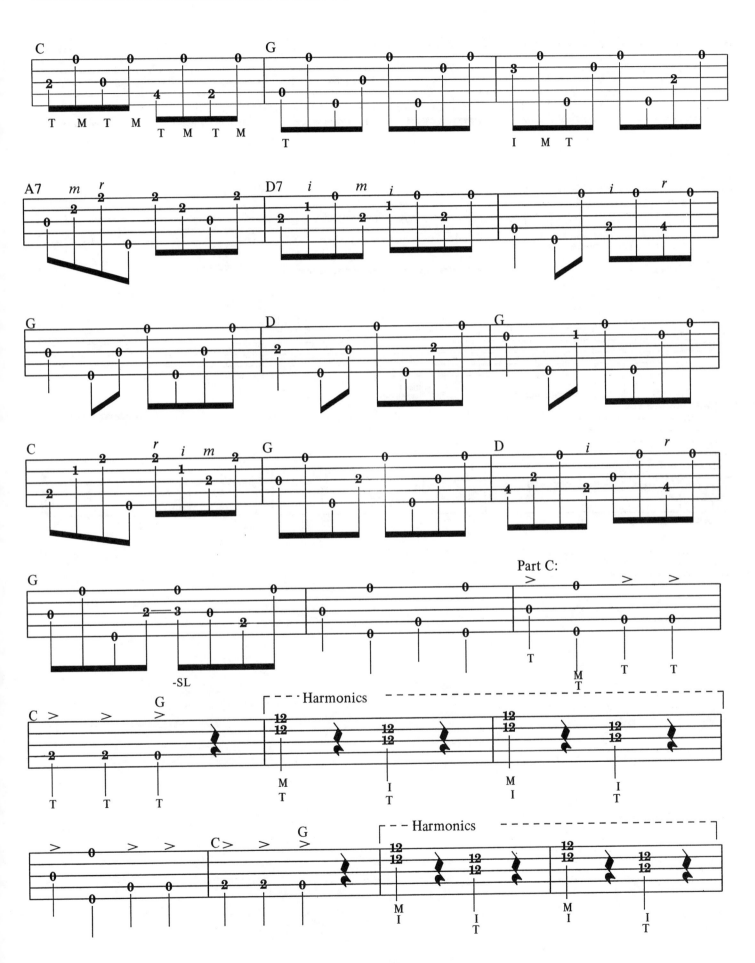

Lesson 35: Using a Capo

"Old Joe Clark" is another well-known bluegrass tune. This song is normally played in the key of A. This simply means that you should place a **capo** across the 2nd fret of your banjo. When you use a capo, the capo becomes the nut. Therefore you should play the song exactly as you did without the capo, but your left-hand position is moved up two frets, due to the capo, and the banjo tones are higher in pitch, putting it in the key of A.

You will also need a separate capo for the *fifth string*. If you don't have a fifth-string capo, you can tune the fifth string to an A (to sound like the first string at the 7th fret). However, you may eventually break the string. It is very important for a banjo player to have a capo and to learn to play the songs which are customarily played in the key of A with a capo.

Fact: Fiddle players, mandolin players, and bass players often learn a song in a specific key. Normally, they know how to play "Old Joe Clark" in the key of A. They also often play "Cripple Creek" in the key of A. The tuning of these instruments makes it smoother and easier to play these songs in this key. Banjo players usually learn these songs without the capo, in the key of G. Then they add the capo on the 2nd fret, so that they are then sounding the pitches which belong to the key of A.

"Old Joe Clark" is divided into two sections, just like "Cripple Creek": Part A, which should be played twice, and Part B, which should also be played twice. This is a common form for many traditional fiddle tunes, as is playing in the key of A. Notice also that this tune calls for a partial F chord:

F

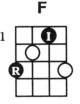

NOTES
---

1. There are many different types of capos on the market. The elastic capo is inexpensive, but it wears out. The Shubb and the Kyser are excellent. Also, for the fifth string, Shubb makes a sliding capo which is easy to use. Many professionals use little railroad tacks on the 7th, 9th, and sometimes the 10th frets in their fingerboard for a fifth-string capo. These are not difficult to install and are available from several bluegrass mail-order companies or from your local music store.

2. You do not have to have a capo to play the following arrangement. However, it is time to begin using your capo if you have one.

• This tune is traditionally played with the capo placed on the 2nd fret, so that you are playing in the key of A.

• Part A consists of two phrases (sentences) of four measures each. The second phrase is similar to the first phrase. This is a common structure in many songs.

Old Joe Clark

(Pick-Up Notes) Part A:

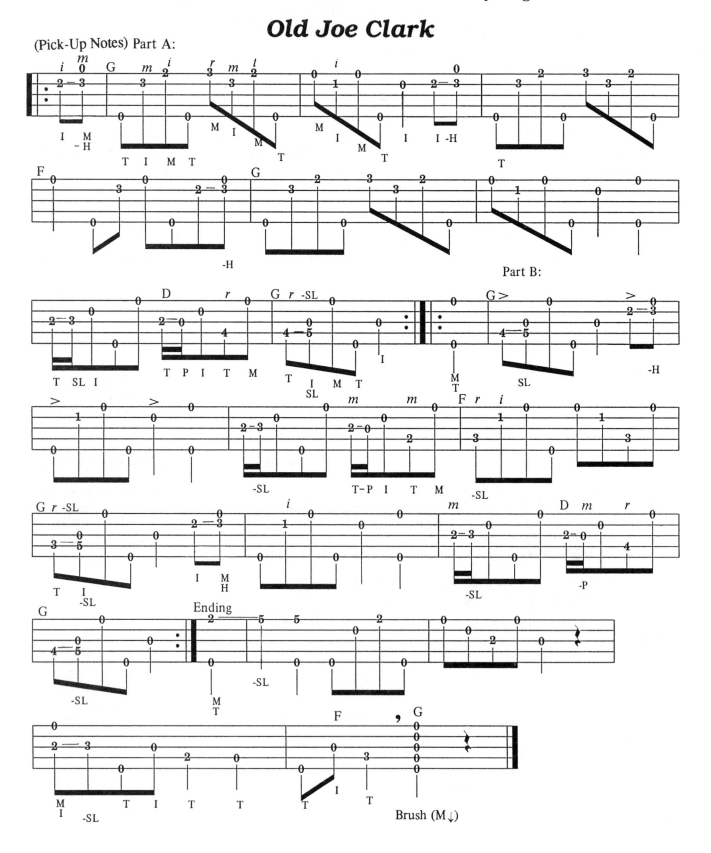

Lesson 36: The F Chord

In Part B of "Old Joe Clark," you may have noticed that you had to hold a partial F chord with your left hand....

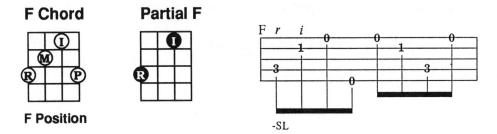

F Chord   **Partial F**

F Position

The *F chord* is common in many *"modal"* tunes. Before the G, C, and D chords were considered standard chords for the key of G, songwriters based their tunes on one of several different scales. One scale, called the **Mixolydian mode,** uses the *G chord* and the *F chord* as the primary chords to provide the harmonic structure. Many tunes which originated in or can be traced to the Appalachian Mountains were based upon this Mixolydian mode. The composers may not have known the scale was a "scale" or a "mode," but they knew the "sounds" of these scales from the songs of their ancestors. "Old Joe Clark" and "Little Maggie" are among these.

This may seem very confusing right now; but one of these days, after you have heard and played many different tunes which use the G and F chords as their primary chords, you will begin to identify this sound and will automatically know which chords to work with when playing your rolls and licks. Again, the term for this *sound* is "Mixolydian."

You may also notice that a D chord occurs in these tunes, also. This was added in later times because people became so used to hearing the D chord that a song didn't sound "right" if the D chord didn't occur before the final G chord. These songs can actually be played with or without the D chord. In fact, some people have omitted the F chord entirely, and play only the D chord where the F chord used to occur. **However,** most people like the modal sound and enjoy using the F chord.

Are you beginning to see, at least a little, that this music is very improvised? That is part of the fun.

The following arrangement is a fairly standard arrangement of "Little Maggie." The same is true of the arrangement you learned of "Old Joe Clark."

The first variation of "Little Maggie" uses the forward roll as the primary right-hand pattern. Hammers, slides, and pull-offs to be sounded by the left hand have been added for embellishment. The complete F chord is held for the third and fourth measures.

Little Maggie
(Mixolydian)

The second variation of "Little Maggie" builds upon the first variation by using more of the left-hand techniques. Try substituting some of the "licks" from this variation into the variation above. For example, substitute #5 and #6 from Variation II for #5 and #6 in Variation I.

Little Maggie
(Variation II)

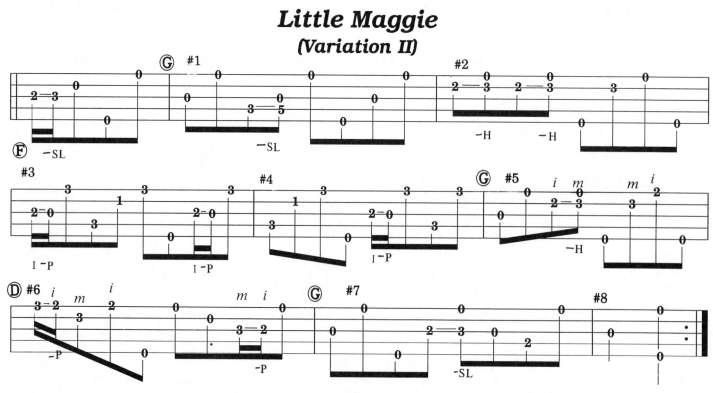

Lesson 37: Old Man at the Mill

This is a great tune which is played in the Mixolydian mode.

• Notice that the main chords are the G and the F chords.

• Notice that it also includes a half measure, similar to the one occurring in "Down the Road." (Accent the first note of this measure.)

• Notice that the sixth measure contains a double pull-off. This is fun to play, and adds a surge to the song without actually speeding up.

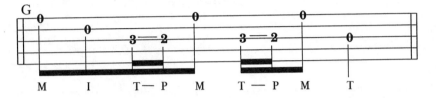

• Notice that the last F chord played uses a new F lick:

F Lick #1

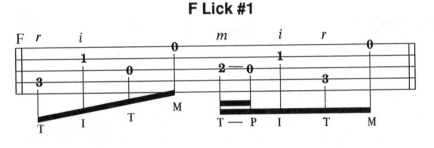

Play this measure for the F chord in any song.

Old Man at the Mill

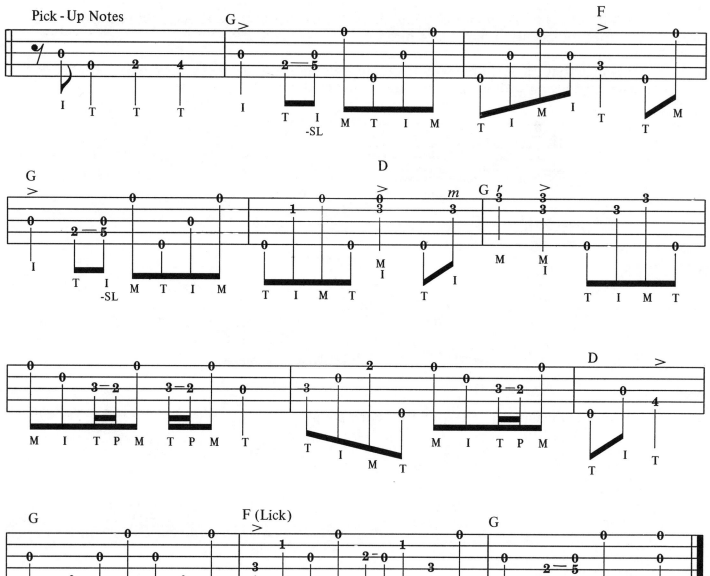

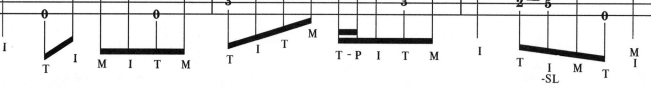

Lesson 38: Pretty Polly

This song sounds better when played with the capo on the 2nd fret. "Pretty Polly" is another modal tune which has been handed down through time. It belongs to the Dorian mode (Gm, B♭ chords), or it can be considered to be in the key of G minor (Gm, C, and D chords). The back-up chords for this are played differently by different bands. Some use the G minor chord throughout, while others throw in a B♭ chord or a D chord where they feel it. There is no precedent for the harmony for this type of song. People still play it the way they feel it.

• Notice that there are quite a few quarter notes in this arrangement. Be sure to hold each quarter note for the duration of two of the eighth notes (regular notes),

e.g. for:

play:

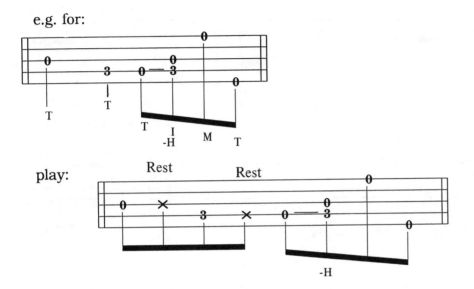

• Also, notice in the third measure that you hammer from 1–3 on the second string and then quickly fret the 3rd fret on the third string,

e.g.

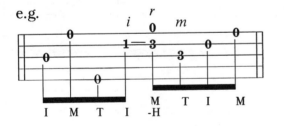

Most people play this tune with the capo on the 2nd fret.

Pretty Polly

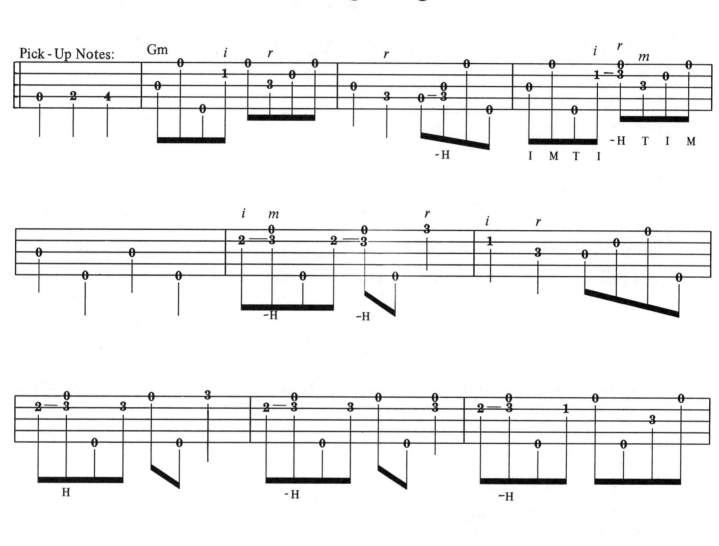

Lesson 39: D Lick #4

"Shady Grove" returns us to the familiar sound of the G and D chords (Ionian mode) upon which most of our familiar traditional music is based. Notice that the G chord is played for almost every measure. Actually, there is only one D lick (which occurs just before the last G chord). This lick can be interchanged with the other D licks you have learned.

D Lick #4

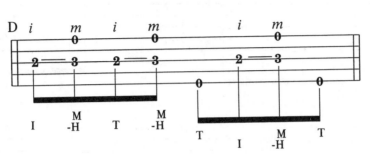

Thumb through the songs in this book and notice how often you find D-chord licks just before the final G-chord licks. This is important. When you start to jam with other musicians, you will know which chords to play as back-up and which licks to use for lead when playing a song that is new to you.

People often use the capo on either the 2nd fret (key of A) or on the 3rd fret (key of B♭) to play "Shady Grove." However, the capo can be placed anywhere you like, for it is a vocal or singing song, and people generally place their capos in a good singing range. (Of course, you don't have to use the capo at all to play it in the key of G.)

Which roll is the primary roll pattern?* Notice that you should emphasize your right thumb to bring out the melody of the song.

—————————————— NOTES ——————————————

*The forward roll: T I M T I M T I.

Shady Grove

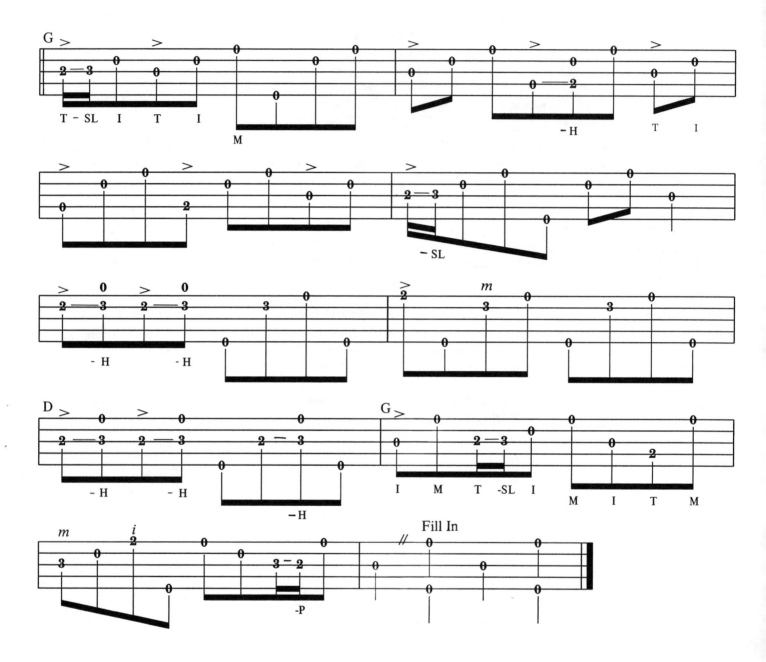

Lesson 40:
Fretting the Fifth String

It is not uncommon to play a note on the fifth string, other than the open G. "Banjo Signal" is fun to play, for the melody is played on the fifth string, while the background notes are played on the other strings. Watch your left-hand fingering carefully.

Banjo Signal

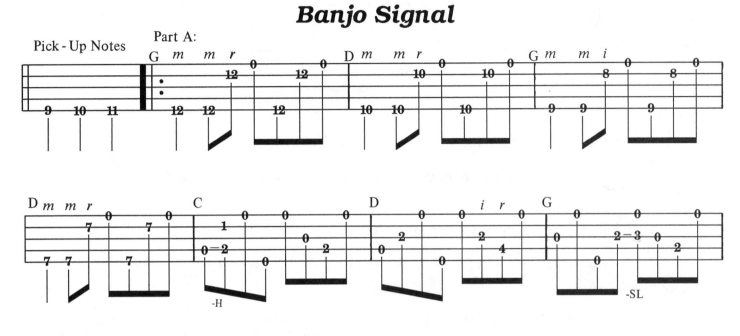

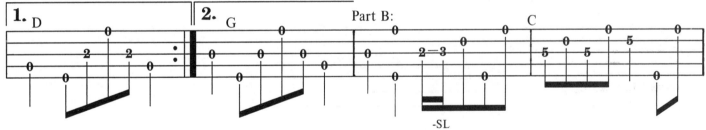

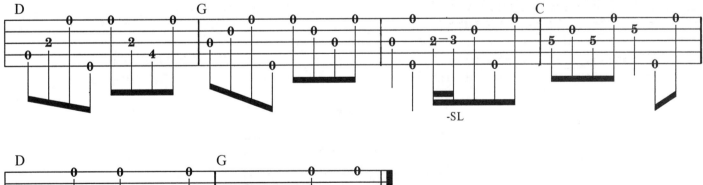

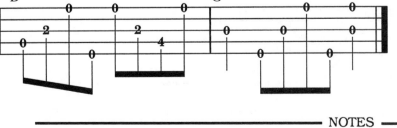

NOTES

The left *middle* finger frets the fifth string in the first four measures.

Lesson 41: The Choke

The up-the-neck arrangement of "Lonesome Road Blues" introduces a new left-hand technique called the **choke,** sometimes referred to as "bending the string." In the third measure of the following arrangement, play the choke as follows:

G Lick (Using the Choke)

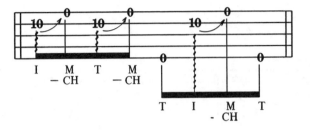

1. Fret the 10th fret with the left middle finger, and pick the string.

2. *Then* bend the string with your left finger to raise the pitch. *Really bend it!* It won't break.

3. Pick the open first string while you bend the second string.

4. Pick the string for the next 10; bend the string for the arrow (♪). Pick the open first string when you bend the second string.

Hint: It will help you to play through this measure with the right hand only, playing open strings without using your left hand. What roll is played here? *(This is the Foggy Mountain roll.)*

Drop-Thumb Roll

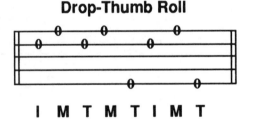

I M T M T I M T

The following is an *up-the-neck lick,* which is used in songs the same way the G Lick #1 is used (the first lick you learned).

Hint: Hold the Em-chord position with your left hand (Cumberland Gap position). Use your left pinky to fret the 11th fret. This lick and G Lick #1 are interchangeable. Try it!

G Lick

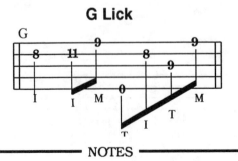

NOTES
---

1. Pick up the basic melody in this arrangement, and compare it to the previous arrangement of this song.

2. Return to "John Hardy (Up the Neck)." Notice the final G lick (p. 53).

Lonesome Road Blues
(Up-the-Neck Arrangement)

Substitute Lick

(Uses three strings of the chord.) Use the proper left-hand fingering.

Lesson 42: Melodic Style

All songs which are played on the banjo use a *scale* as the basis. However, in Scruggs style, because you are using the roll patterns and licks, you may not be as aware of scales as you are of chords.

In the early 1960s, a banjo player named Bill Keith came up with the idea of playing the banjo in the style of the fiddle, playing the same notes a fiddle player might use . . . especially when playing fiddle tunes. This style of playing is based upon playing scales more than chords.

This style has been called Keith style, fiddle style, melodic style, chromatic style, and a multitude of names. However, today it is generally referred to as **melodic style** because virtually every note played is a melody note.

The challenge of playing in the melodic style is that mistakes are very obvious, especially if a wrong note is played. In Scruggs style, the song has a melody which is supported by background notes based upon the chords of the song. The left hand generally works from chord positions. If you pick a wrong note, you are frequently safe because another tone belonging to the same chord will still sound OK. However, in melodic style, you are working along a scale line, rather than from chord positions, and almost every note is a melody note. If you pick a wrong note, it will be more obvious.

What Is a Scale?

The word **scale** comes from the Latin word *scala,* which means *ladder.* If you rearrange each of the notes in a song in order from the lowest pitch to the highest pitch, you will have the scale which is used for that song. This is a fairly simple explanation, but scales actually are fairly simple. Not only does the melody of the song use these notes in whatever order the composer decides, but the chords which are used for the song are also comprised of the scale tones. In other words, the scale consists of the notes which are used to sing and/or play a song. The scale is presented in an ascending or descending order of pitch.

Melodic Style?

Arrangements played in this style work along the scale line. Left-hand positions will hold notes belonging to the scale line, usually in pairs, rather than chord positions. The right hand may or may not play a roll pattern. The right hand is more flexible in this style to be free of the rhythmic right-hand patterns. However, you will find the rolls are also used by the right hand in the melodic style of playing.

EXERCISE: *The first example of this style was the second arrangement of "Cripple Creek." Remember? Look at that variation and notice the left-hand positions. Then return to this section and compare the left-hand positions of these songs. You will see many of the same fret numbers because they all use the G scale (next page). Practice playing this scale, and the melodic style will seem much more familiar as you play through the songs.*

Lesson 43: The G Major Scale

The G major scale is the foundation for most bluegrass songs played on the banjo because each string of the banjo is tuned to the first, third, or the fifth note of the G scale (G, B, or D). The banjo is tuned with the tones which make up the G chord. (Obviously, this is why the tuning is referred to as G tuning.)

In other words, many songs which are played on the banjo are played in the key of G. The key of G simply means a song uses the G scale as its basis. Obviously, it is easier for a banjo player to play the banjo in the key of G (using the G scale) because he can play more open strings.

EXERCISE: *The basic G scale. Play each note on a different string.*

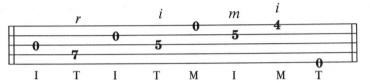

EXERCISE: *Extending the G scale up the fingerboard from the open position to the 12th fret and back.*

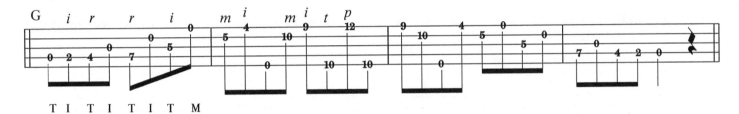

EXERCISE: *Playing a circular scale using the G scale tones. Notice that the first note of each group of four notes walks up the scale line. Many melodic licks use this pattern!*

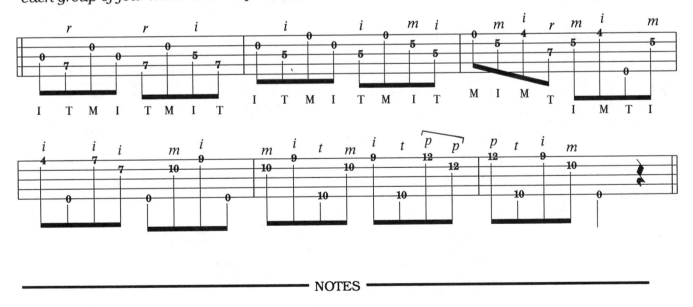

NOTES
---

1. A song in the key of C will use the C scale.

2. Each major scale uses the same fingerboard (fret) pattern along one string. It just begins with a different note.

3. The middle finger of the right hand will occasionally be required to pick the second string.

Lesson 44: Fiddle Tunes

Tunes which are well known for being played on the fiddle can also be played on the banjo. The melodic style is well suited to fiddle tunes. "Devil's Dream" is a very popular fiddle tune which is played on the banjo in this style:

• Once you have learned it, use your capo on the 2nd fret, which puts it in the key of A.

• Watch the left-hand fingering. If you have practiced the G scale, your fingering should feel more natural.

• Play Part A twice; then Part B twice. Then add the ending.

• If a passage is difficult for you to play, isolate it and play it over and over like an exercise. This is a very effective practice technique:

e.g.: m. 3

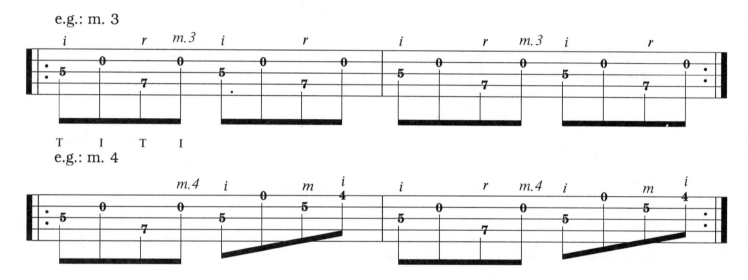

e.g.: m. 4

Then back up, and try to fit the passage with the notes before and after it.

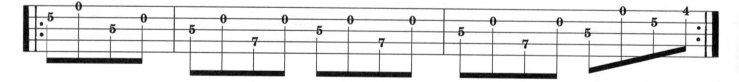

Also, note the fourth measure of Part B uses the pinky on the first string:

EXERCISE:

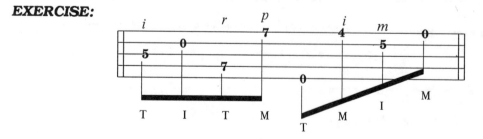

Devil's Dream
(Melodic Style)

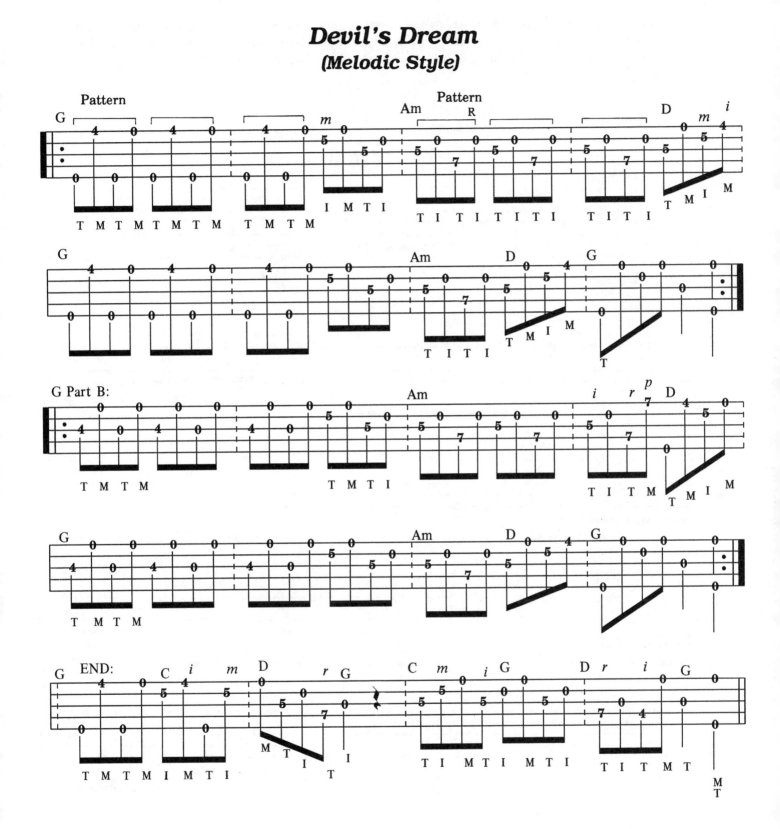

Lesson 45: Turkey in the Straw

Compare the left-hand positions to the G-scale positions — expanding the fingerboard. Watch your left-hand fingering. Usually you will hold down two notes with your left hand. Also, notice the quarter notes; be sure to pause. Notice that Part B begins with the forward-roll pattern.

Turkey in the Straw
(Variation I)

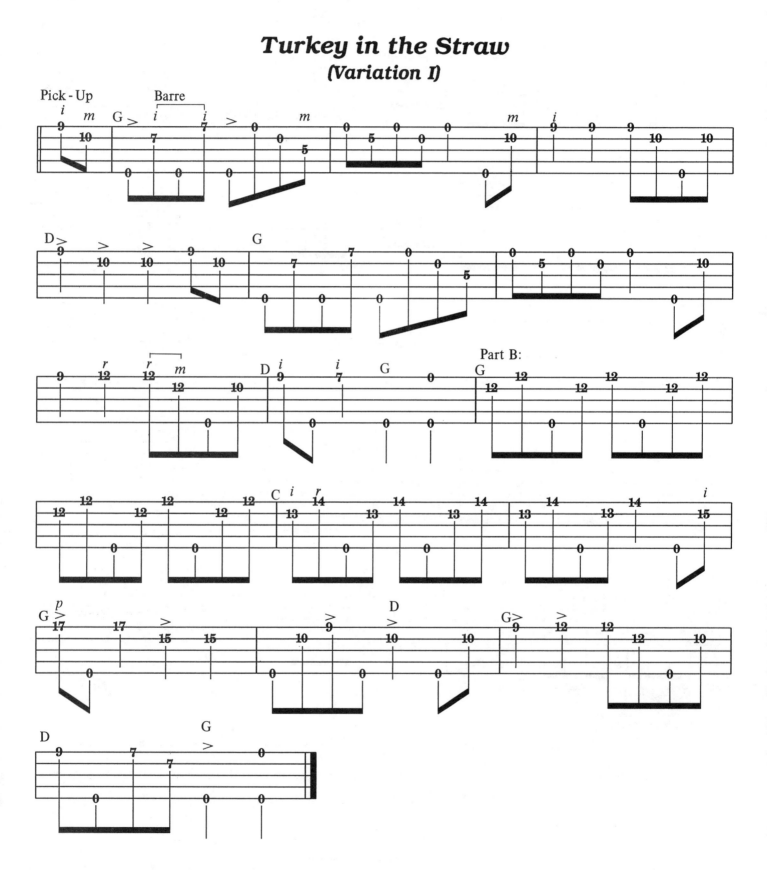

This arrangement builds upon the previous arrangement by adding more notes. Notice that the ring finger frets the fifth string in the third measure.

Turkey in the Straw
(Variation II)

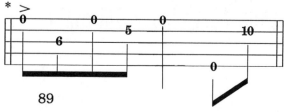

NOTES

*Substitute for measure 2: There are many different possibilities for filling in around the melody notes.

Lesson 46: Blackberry Blossom

Blackberry Blossom
(Melodic Style)

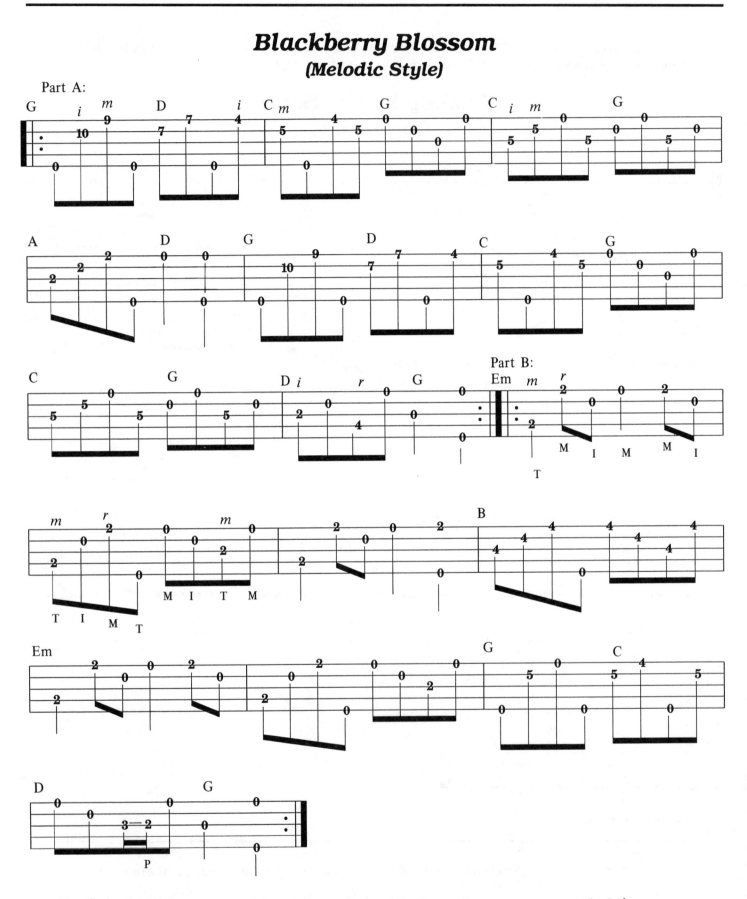

For fun, play this as a second variation, along with the earlier arrangement (p.31).

Lesson 47: Flop Eared Mule

Notice the repeat sign at the end of Part A. (Play Part A twice.) Watch for and *emphasize* the quarter notes. They are important in this tune.

Flop Eared Mule

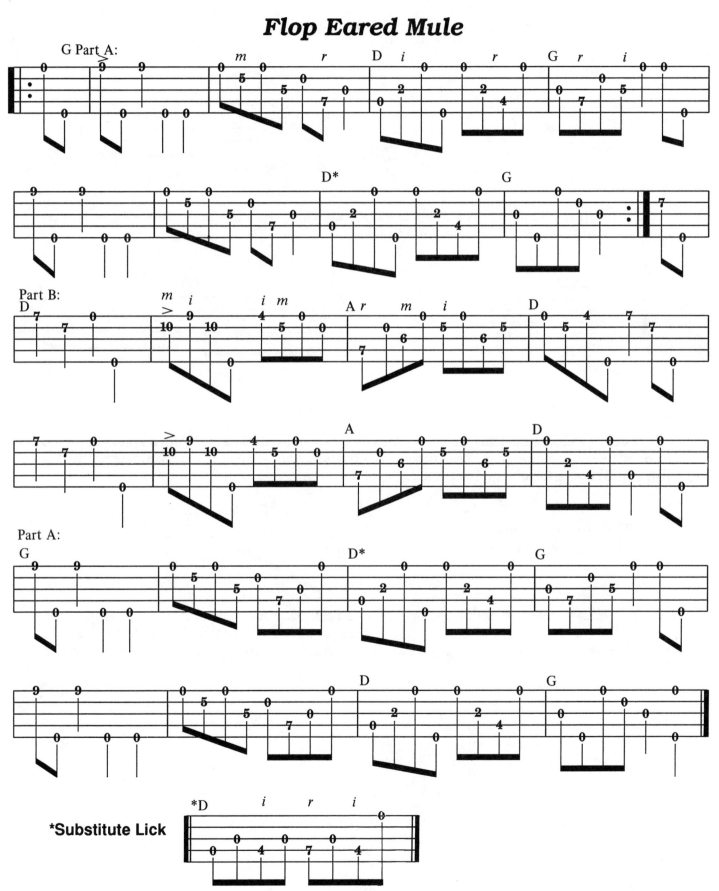

*Substitute Lick

Lesson 48: Sugarfoot Rag

This is another tune fiddlers and banjo players like to play.

Part B introduces a new technique which involves picking the same string twice in a row, using a different right-hand finger for each note. The **single-string technique** has become extremely common among contemporary banjo players,

e.g.:

G Lick

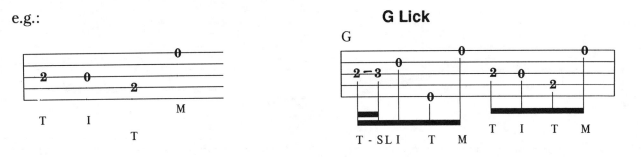

Part B also calls for picking the second string with the right *middle* finger. This is also fairly common but may take some practice,

e.g.:

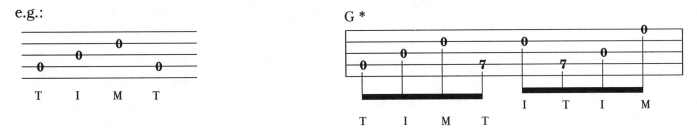

*This is a variation of which roll pattern? *(The forward roll.)*

The introduction: The last three notes of the introduction use triplets as pick-up notes into Part A. You should play these three notes in the same amount of time you normally play two eighth notes (or one quarter note).

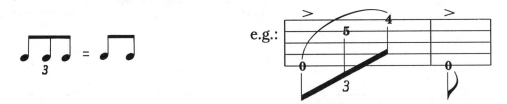

To feel the accent or emphasis, say "TRI-PO-LET" (one syllable per note), and emphasize the "TRI." When you play the triplet, you should also play the note that follows it. You should not stop after the last note of the triplet. In other words, you actually play four notes: the triplet + the next note.

Sugarfoot Rag

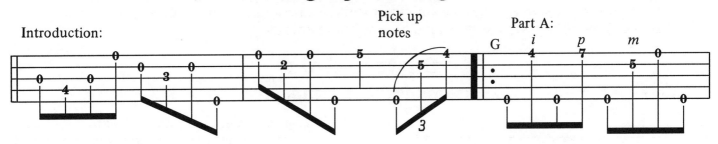

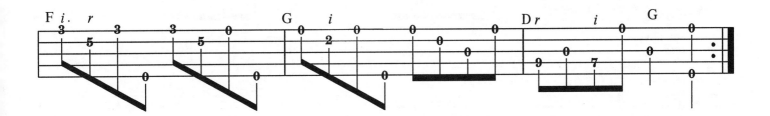

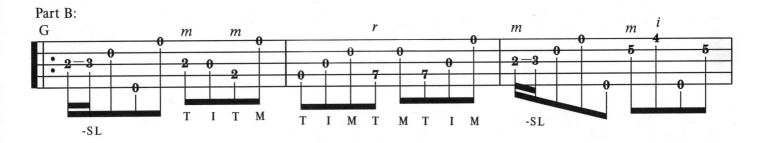

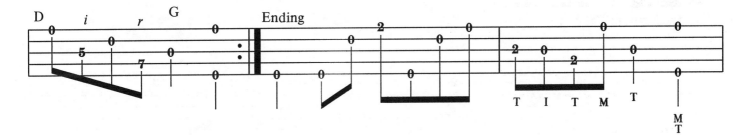

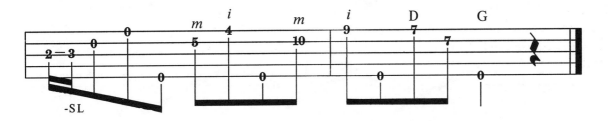

For the pick-up notes, play three notes in the same amount of time two eighth notes are played:

Lesson 49: Buffalo Gals

Actually, any tune can be played in either the melodic style, by playing scale tones for the notes which fill in between the melody notes, or in Scruggs style, using chord tones to fill in between the melody notes. The following arrangements demonstrate two different ways to play "Buffalo Gals." (Each version includes a verse and a chorus.)

Buffalo Gals
(Scruggs-Style Arrangement)

Lesson 50: Buffalo Gals

Accent the index finger in the first two measures to bring out the melody.

Buffalo Gals
(Melodic Variation)

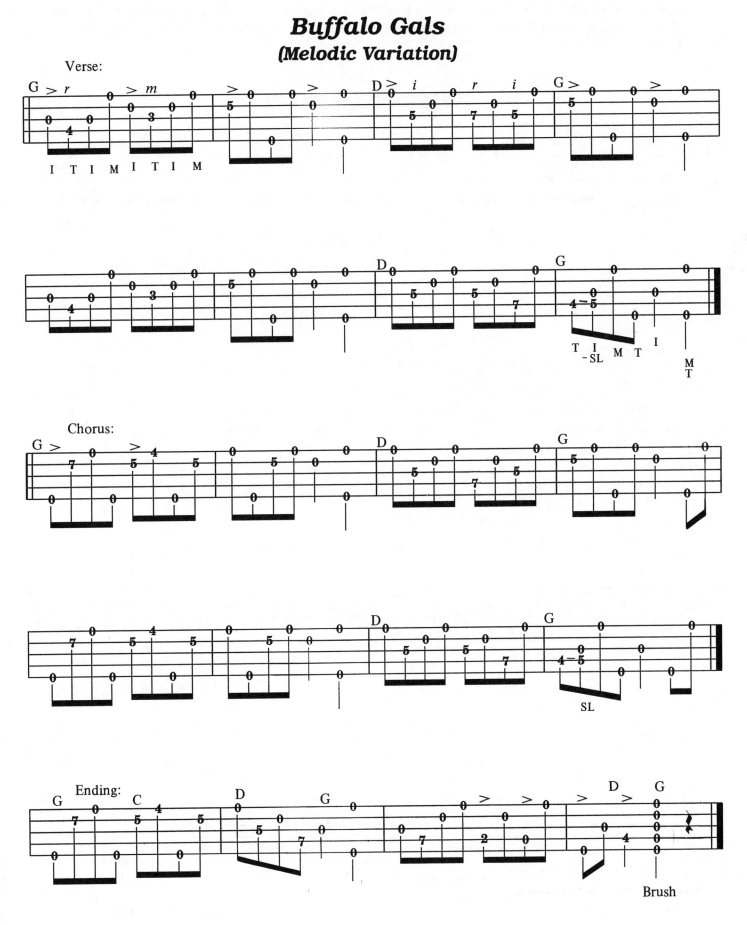

Lesson 51: Wildwood Flower

Once banjo players become skilled in both the Scruggs and the melodic styles, they often find that they like to *combine* or mix the two in a single song. The following arrangement uses *Scruggs style for Part A* (notice the rolls and licks) and a *melodic run for Part B* (notice the scale line).

Wildwood Flower

Part A:

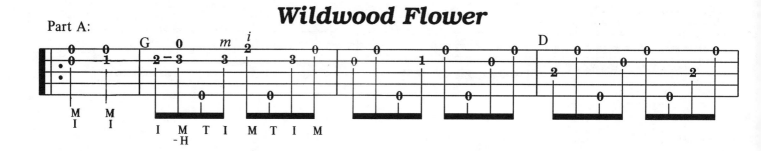

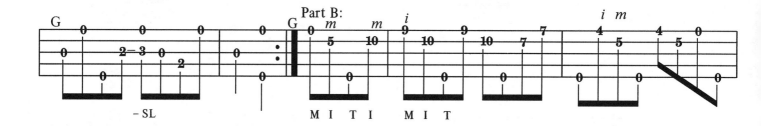

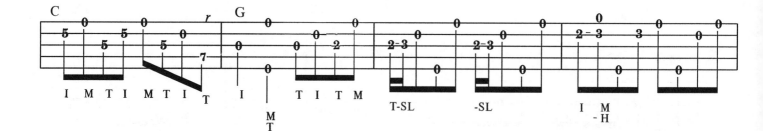

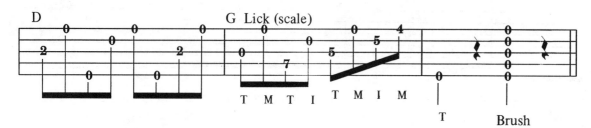

96

Lesson 52: Chord Positions

When playing the banjo in Scruggs style, it should be fairly obvious by now to pay special attention to the chord symbols above the tablature. These tell you which chord position to hold with the left hand, and they also tell you which licks will work when improvising or working out your own arrangement for a song.

Because the banjo is tuned to a G chord, the chord positions in the first position (up through the 4th fret) often leave open strings. However, as you move up the neck, you will find that songs also work from "closed" chord positions, where your left hand holds all four strings to form a chord.

There are only three major chord positions for the left hand. Where you place each of these determines the name of the chord.

The F Position

You have already run across the F chord in "Little Maggie" and "Old Joe Clark." If you hold the F chord, fretting all four strings, then move your left-hand position two frets higher, you will be playing a G chord. If you move it two frets higher again, you will be playing an A chord:

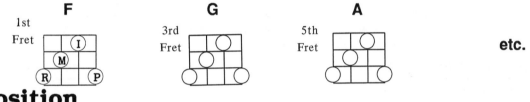

The D Position

Refer to "John Hardy," and you will see that you have worked with the partial D chord. The full D chord is a basic left-hand position which can be held to form any chord, depending upon where you place the position on the fingerboard. (Compare this position with the F position — the index and middle fingers trade places.)

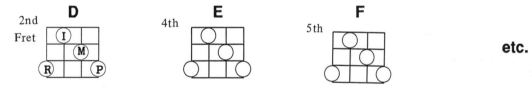

The Barre Position

Remember the first variation of "Blackberry Blossom"? And the A chord in "Salty Dog"? This is the third left-hand chord pattern. You can play any major chord by barring one finger straight across all four strings. At the 5th fret you are playing a C chord. At the 7th fret, you are playing a D chord. At the 12th fret, you are playing a G chord.

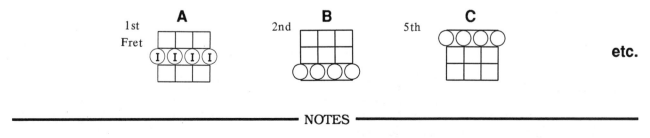

-------------------- NOTES --------------------

The back of this book has complete charts for locations of all of the major and minor chords.

It is important to realize that both lead arrangements and back-up (accompaniment on the banjo when playing along with singing or other instruments) involve playing chords. Try to learn the location of the G chord, the C chord, and the D chord in each of the three major chord patterns. (You will be able to find the location of any other chord from these chord positions, for they work up the scale line alphabetically.)

EXERCISE:

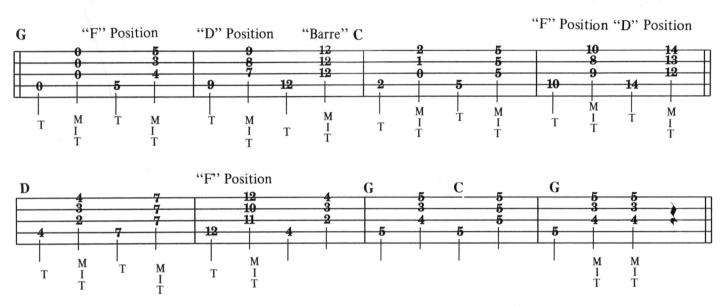

Just for Fun . . . More Exercises

Although the above chords are the most important to learn at this time, the following exercises are also fun to play. These exercises will help train your hands to work together for chords which are often used to play songs in the key of G. (These make great warm-ups.) Your right hand plays which roll pattern?*

EXERCISE: *Using partial chords up the second and third strings. Notice that you are playing a G scale along the third string.*

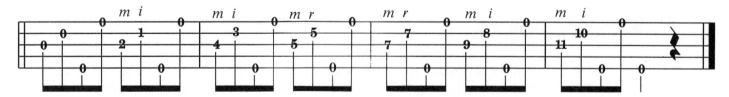

EXERCISE: *Adding the chord tone on the first string so the chord is held on the first three strings. You are now playing G, C, and D chords. These are the primary chords used to play songs in the key of G.*

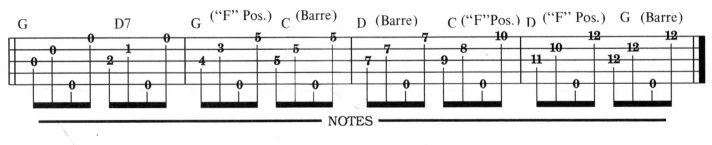

NOTES

*The mixed roll.

EXERCISE: *Just one more for fun.... By changing only the note held on the first string, you can play an entirely different chord. This exercise plays all of the chords which are built with the G scale. These are the chords which are usually used to play songs in the key of G.*

By now you have probably deduced that chords are very important. Keep working on them. It takes practice, but your fingers will learn.

Lesson 53:
Working from Chord Positions

This arrangement requires the left hand to work from chord positions.

Part A:

1. Hold the G chord in the F position. The left ring finger acts as a pivot finger, while the other fingers remain stationary.

 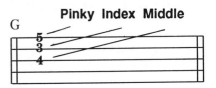

2. Hold the D chord in the D position. Again, the left ring finger reaches the frets which are not in the chord position, while the other fingers remain stationary.

 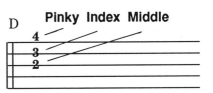

Part B:

Use partial chord positions (two strings) for the G and C chords at the beginning of this section. (However, notice that the G chord is actually a D-position G chord, and the C chord is from the barre position.)

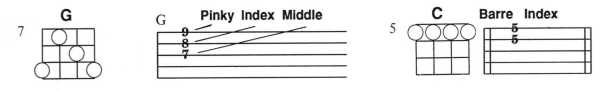

Important: Use your left pinky to fret the first string in the F position and in the D position.

100

Wildwood Flower
(Working from Chord Positions)

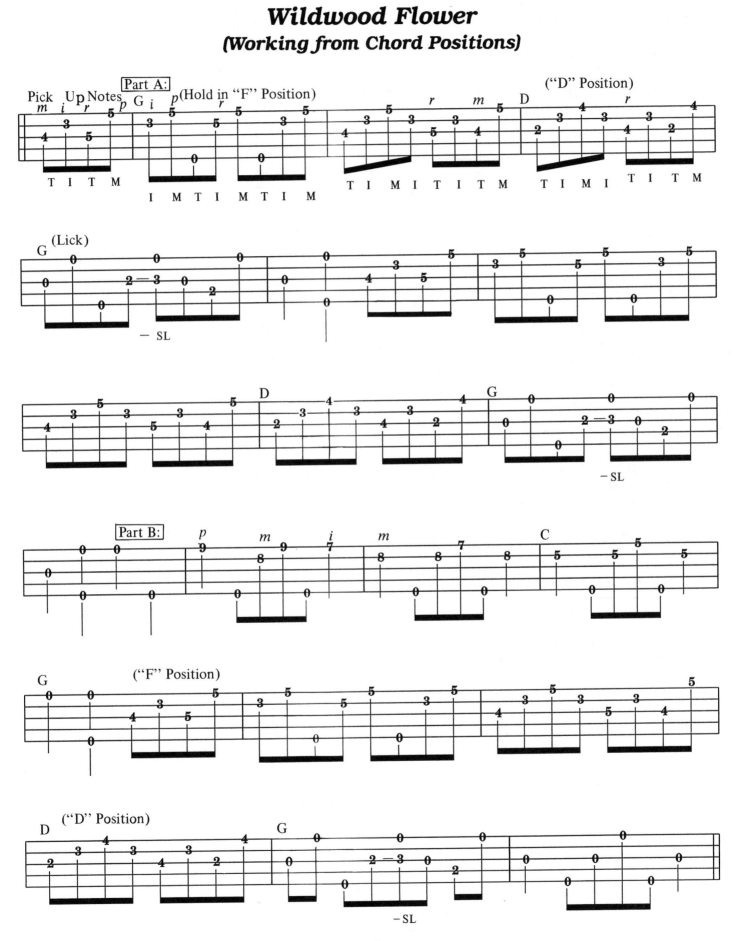

Lesson 54: Two Little Boys

This is a Civil War song about two brothers who fought on opposite sides, and the words tell the story of how the older brother came to the rescue of his younger brother.

When playing through this:

• Notice that the right hand plays the tag roll for almost every measure, generating a rhythm for this section:

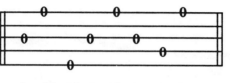

I M T I M I T M

• Play the first ending up to the repeat sign ⌐1.   ¬⌐ 2.   then repeat the song, but substitute the second ending the second time.

• Ending 1 uses which roll pattern for each measure? *(The forward-reverse roll.)*

• In Ending 1, notice that the left hand changes chord positions for each group of four notes:

```
        (G)      (C)    (A)          (C)      (C#)    (D)
A                            D
  7      9       10     11     12     14      15      16
  5      8       8      10     10     13      14      15
  6      7       9      9      11     12      13      14
```

Each measure alternates between an F-position chord and a D-position chord.

Use chord positions with the left hand through the first ending. Play a G scale as the final G lick.

Two Little Boys

Pick-Up Notes

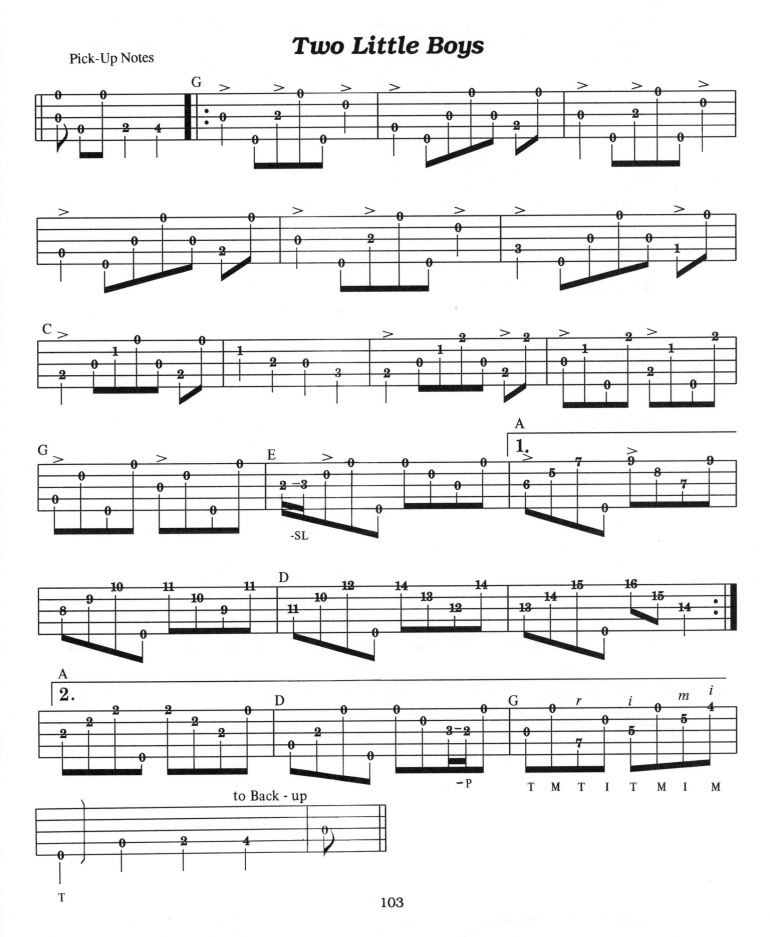

Lesson 55: Waltz Time

Before you begin playing through the following tune, notice that there are only six notes in each measure (or roll pattern). Songs which are waltzes are played in 3⁄4 time, so there are only three beats per measure instead of the usual four beats (eight eighth notes).

When a song is played in 3⁄4 time, you should be able to say: ONE-Two-Three-ONE-Two-Three . . . over and over with the music. The accented notes are the first, third, and fifth notes of each measure. These are the melody notes. (Emphasize the first note the most.)

In waltz time:

• The mixed-roll pattern is played (six notes):

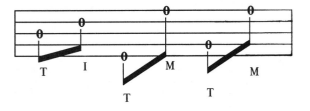

• The forward-roll pattern is played (six notes):

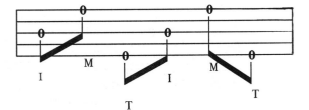

NOTES

You can also vary the roll pattern by using a different picking order. Just be certain to play six notes (or three beats) in each measure. Of course, the quarter note adds emphasis in 3⁄4 time, also. Remember to hold the quarter note for the equivalent time it takes to play two eighth notes.

Emphasize the first note of each measure.

Amazing Grace
(Waltz Time — 3/4)

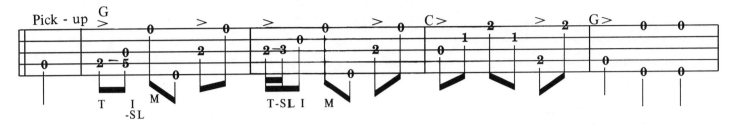

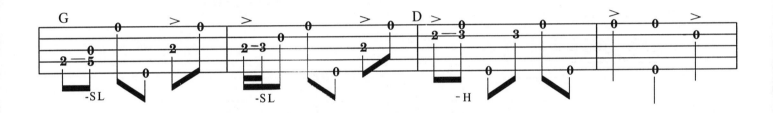

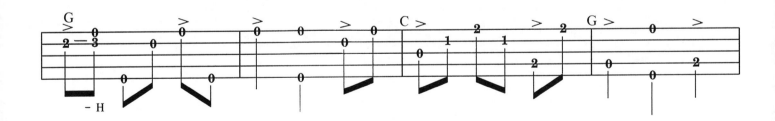

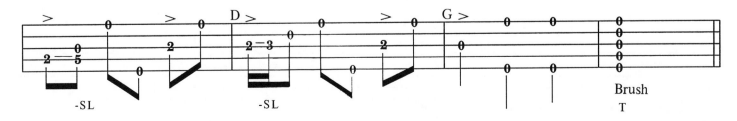

Lesson 56: Silent Night

Have you ever realized that "Silent Night" is a waltz? This song is played in 3/4 time. "Silent Night" is also played in the key of C. This simply means that the chords you will be playing are C, F, and G chords. (Your banjo should stay in G tuning to play this tune.)

Silent Night
(Waltz Time)

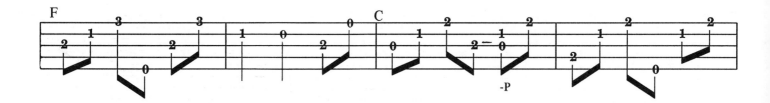

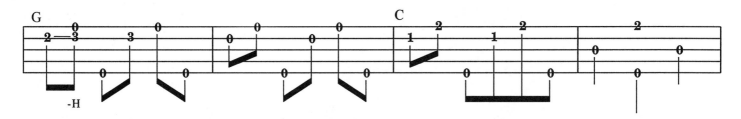

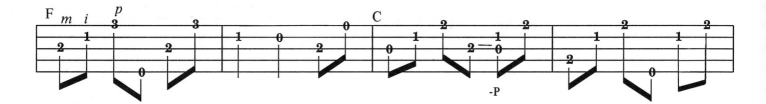

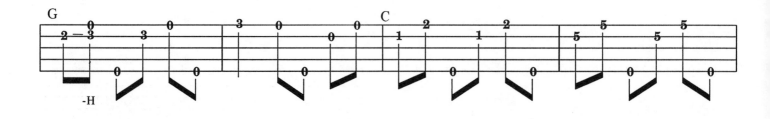

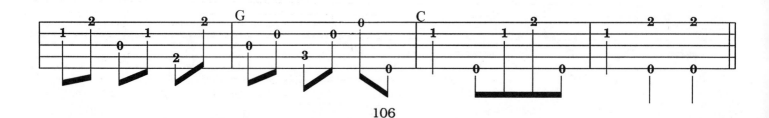

Lesson 57: Home on the Range

This tune is played in the key of G, which means that it works mainly with the G, C, and D chords. However, notice that it also uses some different chords.

Home on the Range
(Waltz Time)

Lesson 58: C Tuning

Do you remember how "Silent Night" was played in the key of C, without altering the tuning of your banjo? I mentioned that the key of C uses the C, F, and G chords as the primary chords. Another way to play in the key of C is to change the tuning of the fourth string (only) of your banjo to a C tone. Lower the fourth-string tuning the equivalent of two frets, *so that when you fret the fourth string on the 7th fret it will sound like the open third string.*

Now your banjo is tuned: **G   C   G   B   D**
                             5th 4th 3rd 2nd 1st

To tune:

1. Tune your banjo to standard G tuning.

2. Loosen your fourth string so that it sounds like the open third string when you fret the fourth string on the 7th fret.

Any song which is played in the key of C can be played in C tuning by retuning the fourth string. This note puts a "bottom" on the C chord.

Your chord positions will be the same, except for the fourth string:

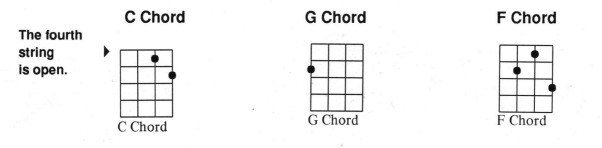

The fourth string is open.

C Chord

G Chord

F Chord

C tuning:

1. Lower the pitch of the fourth string the equivalent of two frets, to a C. (When fretted on the 7th fret, the fourth string should sound like the open third string.)

2. Leave all other strings in standard G tuning.

Soldier's Joy
(C Tuning)

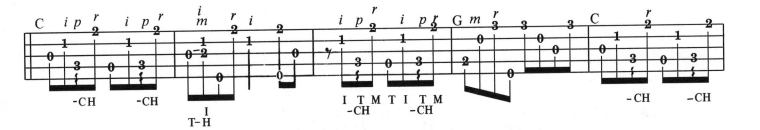

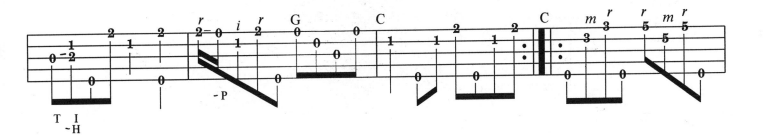

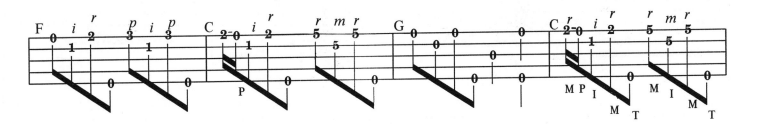

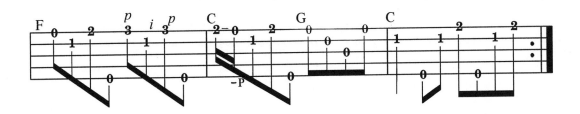

Lesson 59: D Tuning

A beginning banjo book would not be complete without the inclusion of "Reuben." This song is fun to play and uses many of the same techniques used to play previous songs in this book. However, for this tune, the banjo is *tuned to a D chord.* (Many other songs also use D tuning.)

To tune:

1. Tune your banjo to standard G tuning: G D G B D.

2. Lower (loosen) the third string (slightly) until *the open third string sounds like the fourth string on the 4th fret.* This is an F♯.

3. Lower (loosen) the *second string* until it *sounds like the fourth string on the 7th fret.* This is an A.

4. Lower (loosen) the *fifth string* (very slightly) until it *sounds like the first string on the 4th fret.* This is an F♯.

5. The fourth and first strings stay the *same* . . . do not alter these strings.

Your banjo should now be tuned to the following notes:

F♯	**D**	**F♯**	**A**	**D**
5th	4th	3rd	2nd	1st

The fun part about playing in D tuning is that you can use many of the same licks you played in G tuning, and they still work!

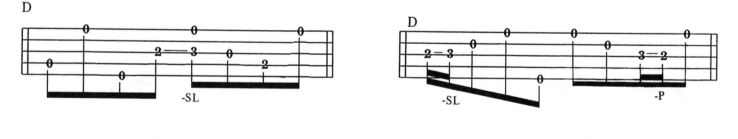

NOTES
---

1. If you have trouble retuning your banjo, electronic tuners are available, and they are wonderful! A chromatic auto-tuner will tell you when you are playing the right note, and if it is perfectly in tune.

2. Also, Keith tuning pegs are available which can be tuned to both G and D tuning. Just turn the peg to the tuning you want. (These pegs have special stops on them, so that you can't turn past the desired note once they are set.)

D tuning:

1. Tune banjo to open-G tuning first.

2. Tune open second string to A; sounds like fourth string at the 7th fret.

3. Tune open third string to F♯ ; sounds like fourth string at the 4th fret.

4. Tune fifth string (lower) to F♯ ; sounds like first string at the 4th fret.

Reuben
(D Tuning)

Key of D:
(D & A chords)

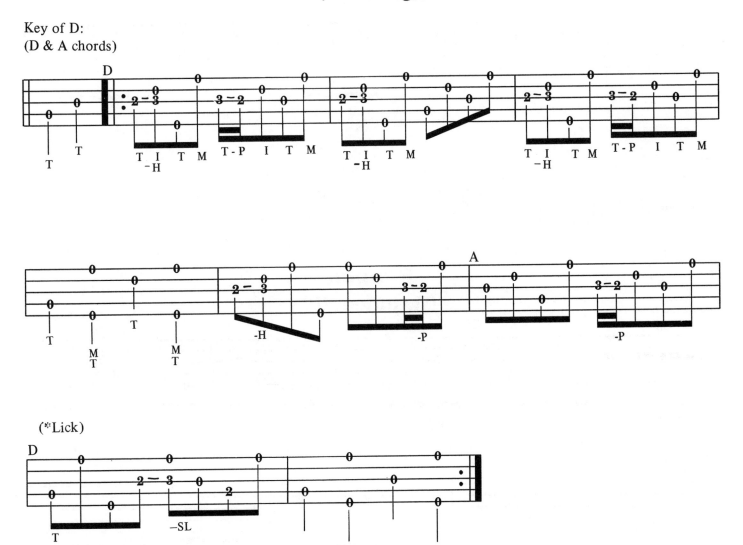

111

Use the choke technique.

Reuben
(Variation II)

Reuben
(Variation III)

Chord Charts

Major chords are formed from the first, third, and fifth tones of the major scale of the chord name. There are three left-hand positions for all major chords.

Major Chords
G Tuning

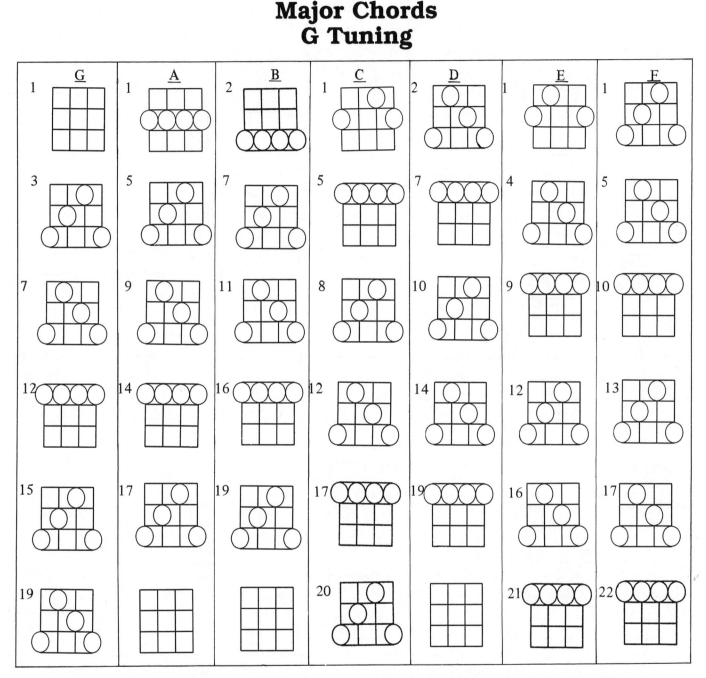

The number beside each diagram indicates the fret number where the chord begins.

Major chords provide the primary chords for songs played in major keys. (Most bluegrass songs fall into this category.) In addition, they can also be substituted for other chords in a song, either to fulfill the function of those chords, or to act as passing chord, or to add color.

Note: ♯ means to "sharp" or raise in pitch one fret. If a ♯ follows the letter name of a chord, the chord should be played one fret higher than the regular position. ♭ means to "flat" or lower in pitch one fret. If a ♭ follows the letter name of a chord, the chord should be played one fret lower than the regular position.

Minor Chords
(Symbol = m)

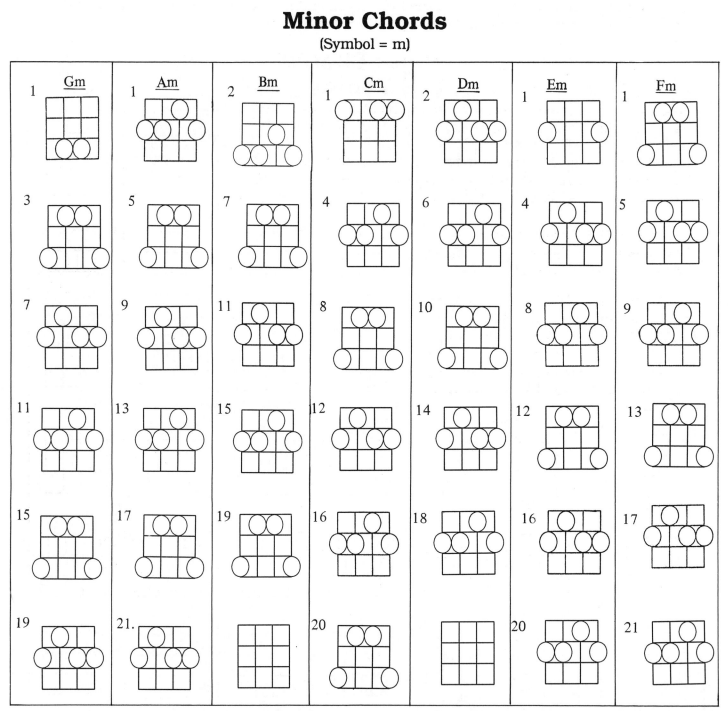

The number beside each diagram indicates the fret number where the chord begins. Minor chords are usually indicated with a letter followed by a small "m."

Note: ♯ means to "sharp" or raise in pitch one fret. If a ♯ follows the letter name of a chord, the chord should be played one fret higher than the regular position. ♭ means to "flat" or lower in pitch one fret. If a ♭ follows the letter name of a chord, the chord should be played one fret lower than the regular position.

Locating Chords Without a Chart

• The chord names change in alphabetical order as each chord position pattern is moved up the fingerboard. (The musical alphabet is A through G repeated over and over.) Notice that B is located next to C and also that E is next to F, but that all other letters are separated by a fret. (The frets in between work like the black keys on a piano.) To locate a specific chord without a chord chart, you can start with one of the chord position patterns, such as the F-position F chord, and move it up the fingerboard until you arrive at the desired chord alphabetically. If you know all of the positions for the G, C, and D chords, you can also find the other chords in relation to these chords. For example, the E chord is always located two frets higher (in pitch) than the D chord.

• ♯ means to "sharp" or raise (in pitch) one fret. Therefore, any chord with this symbol following the letter will be located one fret above the position of the chord letter, i.e. G♯ is located one fret position above the G chord.

• ♭ means to "flat" or lower (in pitch) one fret. Therefore, any chord with this symbol following the letter will be located one fret lower than the regular position for this chord, i.e. B♭ is located one fret lower (in pitch) than B.

• Minor chords, diminished chords, and augmented chords can be located by first locating the normal major-chord position of the desired chord. Each of these chords requires altering a tone of the major chord. (See chart for more explanation.) The following diagrams demonstrate how these chords can be located from the major chord positions.

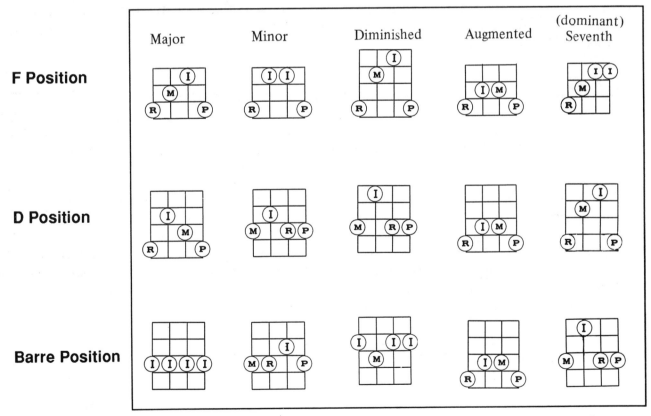

Note: Barre the left index finger across the strings when it is indicated on more than one string in a chord position.

• A number following a chord symbol (i.e. G7 = dominant 7th chord) means that an extra tone is added to the chord. (The major chord can also be substituted for chords of this nature.)

Summary

You should now have a pretty good start at feeling like a banjo player. Where to from here? The next step should be...

• **Splitting the Licks:** This book goes into more detail on the material you have learned in this book. It also shows you how to develop your own arrangements for any song you may want to play, step by step. It covers Scruggs style, melodic style, and also has an advanced section on improvising. Double tapes containing all of the music in the book are also available. (Mel Bay Publications, Inc., P.O. Box 66, Pacific, MO 63069)

• **Back-Up Banjo:** The main objective of this book involves playing with other musicians. You are now ready to begin to learn about back-up. This book has over 30 songs which include a "lead break" (like the ones in this book) and back-up arrangements, as well as detailed instructions and licks pertaining to playing with other musicians. Many teachers also use the songs in this book to provide additional arrangements for their students. The cassette tape covers all of the licks and also features the songs with a full bluegrass band. The tape is in stereo, so that the banjo is on one channel and the rest of the band on the other. (Mel Bay Publications, Inc.)

• **Banjo Handbook:** This compact book is a handy reference guide for banjo players and is especially helpful for beginners. It includes advanced roll patterns, licks, back-up techniques, playing up the neck, many quick and helpful hints, as well as songs for each section. It also includes a step-by-step section on how to set up your banjo for the best tone and playability, and how to fix potential problems — how to change a head, place the bridge, lower the action, etc. This book also has a cassette tape which features the music in the book. (Mel Bay Publications, Inc.)

Also: Two very valuable monthly publications for banjo players:

• For the publication which covers anything and everything concerning banjos, playing the banjo, and banjo players, including regular monthly columns and tablature for a wide variety of songs, write to *Banjo Newsletter*, P.O. Box 364, Greensboro, MD 21639.

• The following magazine covers anything and everything to do with bluegrass music and the people involved in it. Write to *Bluegrass Unlimited*, Box 111, Broad Run, VA 22014.

Above all, it is important to listen to as much music as you can . . . particularly banjo music! The above publications provide many sources for the top bluegrass recordings, as well as reviews on many of the latest recordings and books.